LAND AND
EXPAND

6 Simple Strategies To Grow Your Company's Top And Bottom Line

PATRICIA WATKINS

INDIE BOOKS
INTERNATIONAL®

ISBN: 978-1-952233-18-0
Library of Congress Control Number: 2020915426

Designed by Joni McPherson, mcphersongraphics.com

INDIE BOOKS INTERNATIONAL, INC®
2424 VISTA WAY, SUITE 316
OCEANSIDE, CA 92054
www.indiebooksintl.com

PRAISE FOR *LAND AND EXPAND*

"Patricia Watkins delivers again. Another pragmatic blueprint for sustainable success in an increasingly unpredictable business environment. Land, EXPAND, and succeed!"

Mike Ruffolo, Chairman, Edgeware AB, former CEO, Internap Corporation, Crossbeam Systems, and Liquid Machines

"Among the biggest challenges for a go-to-market organization is limiting churn and expanding its footprint in existing clients. Patricia's book is an excellent roadmap to making this expansion a reality. A must-read for sales leaders in all industries."

Bruce Dahlgren, CEO MetricStream

"This is the best guide to customer retention and revenue expansion I've seen recently. Watkins has produced a thoroughly practical compendium of best practices, backed up by statistical evidence. Few platitudes here. Consider instead, what's the real cost of poor service? Conversely, what's the dollar value of customer retention? Land and EXPAND *is well worth buying just for its quantitative insights on why and how to focus on customer satisfaction for business expansion."*

Ernie von Simson, Cofounder The Research Board; Senior Partner, CIO Strategy Exchange (Retired), author of *The Limits of Strategy: Lessons in Leadership from the Computer Industry* and *Discarded Patriot*

"Patricia Watkins' book Land and EXPAND *is a must read for anyone in sales. It provides six simple strategies in an easy to execute formula for bringing in new accounts and expanding business with existing accounts. It is a customer-focused approach that will help you deliver outstanding customer service."*

Len D'Innocenzo, Founding Partner, Corporate Sales Coaches, LLC, author of *The Agile Manager's Guide to Customer-Focused Selling* with Jack Cullen

"Watkins has just delivered the outlines, research, real-life examples, and direction to expand your sales! Adding the tools and what to do next is what sets her book apart from other sales management books and provides a methodology for increasing sales in your own territory or business. A very good book!"

Scott Schafer, Principal/CEO, SMS Advisors, prior Global VP of Sales for Arecont Vision, Pelco, and Reynolds and Reynolds, Past Chairman, Security Industry Association

"Excellent book—easy to read, great examples, and a great set of strategies to apply to selling in good times and bad. The six battle-tested strategies are based on a proven path to drive sales results."

Dan Doster, Consultant, McKinsey & Company, start-up Paper Water Bottle, author of *Relationships Matter: A Practical Business Guide*

"A direct and detailed roadmap that can help both seasoned and new sales organizations, experienced and growing leaders, and large and small companies to drive top line growth. Land and EXPAND *should be the focus and battle cry of every organization wanting to achieve next-level success."*

Tom Webster, Chief Executive Officer, The TONE Knows, Inc. ("TONE")

"The world of sales is changing and many sales leaders are a deer-in-the-headlights frozen, lost and confused on what to do next. Patricia's simple six-step EXPAND approach is exactly what's needed to bring back some method to the madness. It is based on proven practices for today's modern sellers that will create immediate business impact for creating a repeatable, predictable, and scalable sales engine."

Lorin Coles, Managing Director and Founder, AllianceSphere

"The Pandemic of 2020 caused many companies to focus on recovering sales as quickly and effectively as possible. This book is a must-read to accelerate sales! It shines a light on delighting customers as a sure way to win in the new competitive battleground. I highly recommend this book of six simple strategies to grow your company's top and bottom line."

Theresa Marcroft, President, MarketSavvy, Inc., author of *The Path to Revenue — The Secret of Successful Tech Leaders*

"Land and Expand is a well-developed framework for driving sales and profit. Patricia's experience as a sales leader and her way of articulating the process makes this book a strong roadmap to taking care of your customers. This book will appeal to anyone who wants to establish and build profitable customer relationships."

Jerry Phillips, President, NineRuns, author of *Always Be Looking for Stars: How Leaders Can Hire the Right People with the Right Process* and *Total Assessment: 10 Steps to Smart Recruiting*

"Many companies make the mistake of focusing their attention exclusively on landing new customers. In a slow economy, this can be a lengthy and expensive process. A quicker path to revenue is to meet and exceed the expectations of existing customers; who will stay with you, refer business, and expand their footprint with your company. Patricia's book "spotlights" this quicker path to revenue, (with existing customers). Her six simple, proven strategies, should be in every sales playbook."

Kimberly Layne, Owner and Principal Consultant for KCC: The Kimberly Connection Company, author of *Connections Change Everything: How Smart Leaders Connect Through Better Conversations*

CONTENTS

mom –
to the best mom ever!
Love you
tons –
Patty

PART 1

Choose Growth

CHAPTER 1

Why The Need To Land And EXPAND

"Instead of focusing on the competition,
focus on the customer."[1]
—Scott Cook, CEO, Intuit

Land and Expand has been a best practice for a long time. Given recent events, it is now more vital for your company's success than ever before.

In the first two decades of the twenty-first century, we have experienced several significant events that upended customers' buying patterns and impacted the economy in unprecedented ways. Consider September 11, 2001, when airlines were grounded, the New York Stock Exchange was frozen, and customer confidence was badly shaken. Recall the Financial Crisis of 2008, leaving mortgage holders upside-down, commercial credit hard to obtain, and the stock market taking an extended nosedive. These difficult events caused many buyers to put orders on hold or take longer to make purchasing decisions.

Another significant event was the pandemic of 2020. Customers' buying patterns were impacted in ways that had never been seen before. Schools were closed, travel was

---

[1] https://www.brainyquote.com/authors/scott-cook-quotes

canceled, and people hunkered down. Large companies sent employees to work from home or went into hibernation. Small businesses were temporarily closed or scaled back their products and services. Businesses, large and small, teetered on the edge of extinction. Millions of workers were laid off or furloughed. Confidence cratered, people stayed home, and the old axiom, "business as usual," lost its meaning.

So, what happened? Many companies survived, some did not. A primary factor that ensured survival were loyal customers who continued to purchase from companies during this unprecedented time. Think of the many small businesses, such as restaurants, that were kept afloat by their loyal customer base.

In every significant event, those companies who not only survived but thrived were those who treasured their customers and served them well. Well-served customers reciprocate with loyalty.

During the past, current, or future significant events, your customers are what make the difference in your success.

Existing customers and loyal customers are the foundation of a successful business. You need to have loyal customers to have a solid base to build upon. This book is about creating loyal customers, retaining them, and growing them. Expanding your existing customer base is a vital best practice in good times, and even more essential during the rough times. Focus on expansion within your existing customers and grow your top and bottom line.

What is similar, before and after these economic events, in growing your business' top and bottom line? What do shareholders want to see in assessing a company's value? Growth. What are some of the most productive ways to achieve growth? New customers, high customer retention rates, and more sales to existing customers. Any combination of those adds up to growth.

Loyal customers, and retention of existing customers by delivering an excellent customer experience, were and will continue to be the difference between survival and failure. Existing customers will continue to be the source of the fastest path to revenue and profit growth and the most competitive battleground. The competition for customers will be fierce, as acquiring and retaining customers will be the basis for our future success, even more so than in the past.

Never before in our history has retaining and delighting our current customers been more important to sustain our businesses and survive.

This focus on customers is where the Land and EXPAND Sales Framework will guide you in growing your revenue and profit. This book focuses on the EXPAND strategies of the Land and EXPAND Sales Framework. In these pages, you'll see how expanding sales within your existing customer base is the fastest path to expanding your company's revenue and profit.

What Is Meant By Land And EXPAND?

The term "land" refers to getting a new customer. The term "expand" represents expanding your footprint in that company with new solutions and services. Why is the Land and EXPAND Sales Framework important? During my career, I have never met a company that didn't want to expand its top (revenue) and bottom (profit) line. Therefore, let's start with the premise that every company wants to grow sales. Are you accelerating sales in the most efficient way? This book focuses on the quickest path to growing sales—expanding your market share within your current customers.

Loyal Customers Buy More

Satisfied, loyal customers will buy more products, more solutions, and more services from you. To upsell and cross-sell (covered in Chapter Two: Expansion Revenue), the customer must first experience great service with your company to want to continue doing business with you. But a recent study points out an alarming statistic: "it's a well-established fact that 44 percent of companies have a greater focus on customer acquisition versus 18 percent that focus on retention."[2] This lopsided focus could have dire consequences on your growth trajectory.

You need both acquisition of new accounts and expansion within existing accounts, but many companies' focus is misaligned. A greater proportion of companies are spending more effort looking for new customers than retaining and growing the ones they've already landed! Yes, companies need new customers, but retaining satisfied customers delivers a greater return. Focusing on retention surely deserves equal or more attention. Retaining satisfied customers delivers a greater increase in revenue and profit.

The highest close rates and greatest return on investment (ROI) comes from retaining loyal customers who buy more products and services. Focusing on existing accounts enables companies to expand their market share in those accounts and drive incremental revenue and profit overall.

Why Focus On Existing Accounts

Many companies have a laser-focus on signing new customers. That's important, but are they spending as much or more time on their existing base of customers? Why focus on existing accounts? Let me share some research with you:

---

[2] Khalid Saleh, "Customer Acquisition Vs. Retention Costs – Statistics And Trends," The Invesp Blog: Conversion Rate Optimization Blog, November 11, 2019, https://www.invespcro.com/blog/customer-acquisition-retention/.

- According to research by Bain and Company, increasing customer retention rates by just 5 percent increases profits to anywhere between 25 and 95 percent.[3]
- According to Gartner Group, on average, 80 percent of a company's future revenue will come from just 20 percent of its current customer base.[4]
- *Harvard Business Review* reports that it is anywhere from 5 to 25 times more expensive to acquire a new customer than it is to keep a current one.
- According to the book *Marketing Metrics*, the probability of converting or closing an existing customer is 60 to 70 percent. In contrast, the probability of closing a new customer is 5 to 20 percent.[5]

Focusing on your existing customer base provides the most cost-effective path to growth. Still not convinced?

- Salesforce reports loyal customers, on average, are worth up to 10x as much as their initial purchase.[6]
- Forbes.com reports that an existing customer spends an average of 67 percent more than new customers.[7]

[3] Amy Gallo, "The Value of Keeping the Right Customers," *Harvard Business Review* (Harvard University, November 5, 2014), https://hbr.org/2014/10/the-value-of-keeping-the-right-customers.

[4] Alex Lawrence, "Five Customer Retention Tips for Entrepreneurs," Forbes (*Forbes* Magazine, November 12, 2012), https://www.forbes.com/sites/alexlawrence/2012/11/01/five-customer-retention-tips-for-entrepreneurs/.

[5] Patrick Hull, "Don't Get Lazy About Your Client Relationships," Forbes.com, December 6, 2013, https://www.forbes.com/sites/patrickhull/2013/12/06/tools-for-entrepreneurs-to-retain-clients/#5454cada2443.

[6] Tim Packard, "10 Customer Service Stats and What They Mean for Your Contact Center", Salesforce, January 14, 2015, https://www.salesforce.com/blog/2015/01/ten-customer-service-stats-what-they-mean-your-contact-center-gp.html.

[7] Mike Sands, "The Most Under-Tapped Marketing Opportunity: Existing Customers", Forbes, December 17, 2017, https://www.forbes.com/sites/mikesands1/2017/12/19/the-most-under-tapped-marketing-opportunity-existing-customers/#3a7b40af1ab6

- It has been reported that your current customers are 50 percent more likely to try new solutions.[8]
- According to Forbes.com, it is significantly easier to sell your solutions to your existing customers than to a prospect you don't have a relationship with.[9]

Where would you prefer to spend the majority of your time? Landing new customers is important, but the fastest path to growth is to spend quality time nurturing and EXPANDing your customers after the initial sale.

What Is The Cost Of Acquiring Customers?

Existing customers are less expensive to sell to than new customers. Are you aware of your customer acquisition cost (CAC)? *Harvard Business Review*, as noted above, states that "acquiring a new customer is anywhere from 5 to 25 times more expensive than retaining an existing one."[10] Do your business model and growth plan support those costs?

Consider these costs typically associated with acquiring new customers:

- Marketing costs are incurred to acquire new customers, which include inbound and outbound communications and campaigns, social media, advertising, website, promotions, programs, events, and other costs.
- Sales, marketing, and business development headcount costs of those associates needed to acquire new customers are also included. Be sure to use the fully loaded costs

[8] Khalid Saleh, "Customer Acquisition Vs. Retention Costs – Statistics And Trends," The Invesp Blog: Conversion Rate Optimization Blog, November 11, 2019, https://www.invespcro.com/blog/customer-acquisition-retention/.

[9] Paul B. Brown, "Want to Increase Sales, Target Your Existing Customers." Forbes, January 22, 2014. https://www.forbes.com/sites/actiontrumpseverything/2014/01/22/want-to-increase-sales-target-your-existing-customers/.

[10] Amy Gallo, "The Value of Keeping the Right Customers," *Harvard Business Review* (Harvard University, November 5, 2014), https://hbr.org/2014/10/the-value-of-keeping-the-right-customers.

of your employees. The fully-loaded costs include not only salary but also benefits such as insurance, vacation, employment taxes, office space, laptop, mobile phone, local area network, wireless, software tools, turnover and any recruiting costs, and the list goes on. For example, a resource with a targeted salary of $100,000 may have a fully loaded cost of 2.7 to 3 times the employee's base salary—that's $300,000 per headcount!

Now, if you take those figures and consider the previously quoted statistic that it costs *5 to 25* times more to acquire new customers than to retain the ones you have, you will see the CAC is daunting. Have you built that extra cost into your business model or growth plan? Your accounting and finance departments won't overlook the obvious fact that the lower the CAC is, the higher your profitability.

Each one of these statistics points to the criticality of focusing on your current customer base to grow your business. Selling to existing customers is significantly easier and more profitable than winning new accounts. It is significantly easier to sell to an existing customer because these sales have a lower acquisition cost. You already have contracts in place; you already have developed a trusted relationship; and you will have higher close rates. Ultimately, it is more profitable to sell to existing customers than to acquire and sell to a new customer.

By the way, from a timing perspective, did I mention that customers whose trust you have already earned, tend to buy more than a new customer who might be testing the waters with a smaller initial purchase?

The Land And EXPAND Sales Framework

This book focuses on the Land and EXPAND Sales Framework and how you can implement the framework to grow your business. Some might suggest this framework is only relevant to sales and marketing. However, it doesn't just apply to sales and marketing; this framework applies to every employee in every company—including staff in operations, legal, finance, engineering, manufacturing, and every other employee in a company who has the goal to grow.

Existing customers are the fastest path to improving your top and bottom line. From high-tech companies to healthcare to banking to legal to service companies and more, the Land and EXPAND Sales Framework focuses on six simple strategies to expand your business.

The first step is to land your customers. Before you move on to the next customer, you'll want to be sure to deliver the outcomes that your current customer expects. They purchased your solution to alleviate their pain. Meet the expectations or key performance indicators (KPIs) they partnered with you to provide. It is important to deliver exceptional customer service as the foundation of your relationship with the customer. Once you've achieved a delighted customer, you now have references and proof points that will help you land the next new opportunity. We'll talk more about exceptional customer service in Chapter Three, which focuses on exceptional customer service and overall customer experience.

Once you've landed your customer, now you want to expand your footprint within the account. Once you have a delighted customer, branch out within the account (new solutions and new departments), extending your market presence within that account by leveraging your success.

Expanding is the fastest way to grow, and ultimately accelerates you toward your goal of increasing revenue and profit. Expanding is typically much easier than landing. But expanding still takes a lot of work. This book outlines the six simple strategies to expand your business in the accounts that you've already sold to, i.e., which you've already landed.

One goal of this book is to provide you with a robust body of research to give you a broad and varied view of the background leading to the strategies contained in the Land and EXPAND Sales Framework. A second goal is to provide you with real-life experiences of how the implementation of these strategies resulted in expanded revenue and profit. Lastly, the third goal is to provide you with tips, templates, and checklists that you can put into immediate use in your company.

Go to the next chapter for an overview of the six simple strategies.

CHAPTER 2

Grow With The Land And EXPAND Sales Framework

"Great things are done by a series of small things done together." [11]
—Vincent van Gogh

Before we dig into the details and case studies contained in each chapter, let's define and explain the acronym EXPAND and the six corresponding strategies.

The Land and EXPAND Sales Framework™

---

[11] Emma Brudner, "75 Motivational Sales Quotes to Ignite Your Drive in 2020", HubSpot, https://blog.hubspot.com/sales/motivational-quotes-sales-drive-2015

Let's start with the "E" in EXPAND.

Exceptional Customer Service And Customer Experience

Delivering both exceptional customer service and an overall exceptional customer experience is the foundation for achieving additional business. Companies and all employees who embrace this key strategy have a higher probability of both short-term and long-term success. In this new world of software as a service (SaaS), subscription models, cloud anywhere and everywhere, social media, always-on media, information overload, and lots of competitors all vying for your customers' business, your goal is to avoid customer churn. To keep from losing customers, you must provide not only exceptional service but also an exemplary customer experience. The customer experience encompasses all of the experiences and interactions a customer has with your company.

EXpansion Revenue With Upsell And Cross-Sell

The next strategy, the "X" of The Land and EXPAND Sales Framework, is generating expansion revenue with cross-sell and upsell opportunities. Understand your market and your customer's additional needs and how to help them solve those needs as well as or better than the competition. Focus on ways that you can expand your footprint by assisting your customer in solving additional business problems.

Would you like an extended warranty with your order (cross-sell)? Would you prefer fancier sports tires instead of the factory-installed tires (upsell)?

There are many methods to communicate upsell and cross-sell opportunities or campaigns to your customers. One method is via promotions and programs.

Promotions and Programs

The "P" strategy of The Land and EXPAND Sales Framework is to get the word out in the form of promotions and programs. You want to make your existing customer base aware of the additional problems you can help them solve. You need to deliver ongoing messaging through promotions and programs to communicate how you can address key business problems.

Promotions and programs can run the gamut from buy one, get one free, or buy at a special discount, bundled offers, try-it-and-buy-it programs, early adopter programs, loyalty programs, reseller programs, user groups and customer advisory boards (CABs), and many others. The focus is not on discounting but on creating awareness and preference for your solution, and, where possible, a compelling event. Communicate. Communicate. Communicate. Let your customers know the breadth of the problems you solve.

Account Business Plans And Quarterly Business Reviews

The "A" strategy of the Land and EXPAND Sales Framework is Account Business Plans (ABPs) and Quarterly Business Reviews (QBRs).

On an ongoing basis, you need to gather continuous intelligence around your customer's business so that you can better understand and fulfill their needs.

In addition to regular communications, there are two key ways to get a deeper understanding of your customer's business—ABPs and QBRs.

ABPs are created by the sales team to give themselves and the rest of the team an overview of the account to ensure everyone has a more thorough understanding of the customer, their key initiatives, and where the team can better meet the customer's needs.

QBRs are conducted with the key stakeholders of your accounts, keeping both parties aware of each other's plans, and provide the benefit of positioning you better than the competition as a strategic and trusted advisor.

Net Promoter Score And Customer Satisfaction Surveys

The next strategy of the Land and EXPAND Sales Framework is "N"—conducting Net Promoter Score (NPS) and customer satisfaction (CSAT) surveys. Be sure to ask your customers to give you a report card on how you are doing. Make sure to ask your customers informally and formally what they think of your solutions and services and how you are meeting and supporting their needs. Gather their feedback with both NPS and CSAT surveys.[12] Ask your customers how you are doing and not only do something about it but be sure to communicate to your customers your progress and commitment to exceeding their expectations.

Delight Your Customers Daily

The "D" strategy is to delight your customers daily. Bottom line: success starts with exceptional customer service

---

[12] The main difference between CSAT Surveys and NPS is CSAT is typically used to measure short-term customer loyalty while NPS is used to evaluate long-term customer loyalty. "Measuring Customer Experience: CSAT vs NPS Surveys," QuestionPro, October 9, 2019, https://www.questionpro.com/blog/csat-vs-nps-surveys/.

and is reinforced as you delight your customers daily. One bad experience can end a great relationship. Businesses today successfully expand their revenues and profits based on their ability to exceed customer expectations. One of my favorite books, *Raving Fans* by Ken Blanchard and Sheldon Bowles, states, "Just having satisfied customers isn't good enough anymore. If you really want a booming business, you have to create Raving Fans."[13] Blanchard coined the term "raving fan" to describe a customer who is so overwhelmed and floored by the customer service they've received that they can't stop telling everyone about it.[14]

Referral Selling

You'll notice in the Land and EXPAND Sales Framework that the "E" (Exceptional Customer Service and Customer Experience) and "D" (Delight Your Customers Daily) link to referral selling. Providing exceptional customer service and an exemplary customer experience leads to delighted customers, and delighted customers provide references, enabling you to expand your footprint in existing accounts by referral selling. Referral selling has the highest probability of closing the sale over all other sales strategies. To earn referral sales, keep your foot on the gas of delivering an exceptional customer experience and continually focus on delighting your customers.

---

[13] Ken Blanchard and Sheldon Bowles. *Raving Fans* (New York: HarperCollins, 1993), https://www.harpercollins.ca/9780688123161/raving-fans/.

[14] Tyson Downs, "How to Create Raving Fans with Legendary Customer Service." Zendesk, June 19, 2018, https://www.zendesk.com/blog/create-raving-fans-legendary-customer-service/

> *"The key is to set realistic customer expectations, and then not to just meet them, but to exceed them—preferably in unexpected and helpful ways."*
>
> — RICHARD BRANSON [15]

Journey-To-Success Stories

At the beginning of each chapter, I will share an example of how I applied each of the six strategies successfully. I learned many lessons over many years through hard knocks and brilliant leaders. I learned the importance of applying these six strategies consistently and successfully over several decades. By sharing these stories with you, my goal is to shorten your journey to EXPANDed sales.

Summary

The following chapters provide details of each strategy of the Land and EXPAND Sales Framework: six simple strategies to grow your top and bottom line.

If you execute these six strategies, you will EXPAND your sales. This is not the job of one person or one team. Everyone in your company, every single employee, can make a profound difference in the success of your company's growth.

In the next chapter, we'll dig into the "E" strategy of Exceptional customer service and customer experience.

---

[15] "Best Quotes of All Time", Pakwired, https://pakwired.com/best-quotes-of-all-time/the-key-is-to-set-realistic-customer-expectations-and-then-to-not-just-meet-them-but-to-exceed-them-preferably-in-unexpected-and-helpful-ways-richard-branson/

PART II

How To Use
The Six Simple
Strategies To Grow

CHAPTER 3

E Is For Exceptional Customer Service and Customer Experience

"If there's one reason we have done better than our peers in the internet space over the last six years, it is because we have focused like a laser on customer experience."[16]
—Jeff Bezos, founder of Amazon

The most important strategy to expand sales is to provide exceptional customer service and an overall exceptional customer experience. This strategy is the foundation that all the other strategies are built on. Exceptional customer service, which contributes to a stellar customer experience, is the cornerstone of the other strategies.

Journey To Success

Let's look at a company whose solutions were best-in-class. It had an awesome, award-winning solution. In head-to-head competitions, its solutions won. It had marquee customers, and analysts all touted its solutions. Worldwide, its revenue was over $1 billion, and it was on a rapid upward trajectory.

---

[16] https://quotefancy.com/quote/1093259/Jeff-Bezos-If-there-s-one-reason-we-have-done-better-than-of-our-peers-in-the-Internet

One of its sales teams, however, was struggling to meet its quota. In fact, the team was dead last in sales results across fifty United States sales teams. The sales results were so bad that company executives initially joked about firing the whole team and putting the group's salaries in a money market, joking that would yield better returns.

Bob was a successful senior vice-president of sales, and his regions regularly made quota and regularly attended the annual sales trips for high-performing teams. He was highly regarded in the company for consistently delivering results. When the company went through its annual reorganization, territory lines were redrawn, and entire regions were moved to new leadership. Bob drew the unlucky straw, and one of the regions he acquired was this team in last place. Having a disastrous team would potentially throw a wrench in his track record.

When the prior leader of the challenged sales team moved to a new role, Bob asked me if he and I could work together to right the ship.

The first thing I noticed was this team only had a few large prospects in the funnel. The largest opportunity was being led by an aggressive sales rep who clearly didn't need, from his perspective, any help from anyone else in our company, and who was confident we'd win; because after all, our company had the best solution. Everyone, from sales to executive management, thought this deal was going to close. That confidence gave Bob and me some optimism in taking on the team. We still had a long road ahead of us, but at least we'd get off to a good start.

Shortly after I accepted, we learned from the prospect that we'd lost this sale, the largest deal in our pipeline, to a competitor.

It was time for a serious post-mortem analysis to determine where the team had gone adrift and whether the deal was recoverable.

Bob and I gathered a team of internal resources, including technical, architectural, service, and industry experts, all who had previously been kept at arms-length but were standard members of a typical sales team.

We spent days with the group, strategizing about what we could do to win the business back. In our analysis, we hadn't exhibited our ability to provide exceptional customer service to meet the needs of the prospect. We hadn't shown them our breadth of expertise or our capacity to solve their service problems quickly and completely. The customer wanted a direct line to an executive on our team to ensure this mission-critical solution stayed on track.

In our strategy sessions, we outlined the customer's needs and wants and detailed how we could excel in delivering their results, one line item at a time. We assigned an extended tiger team of experts to provide exceptional customer service to meet the prospect's needs during pre- and post-production. We assigned an executive sponsor to establish direct communications between our top executives and the prospect's executive team.

We also put together 24/7 priority one support to resolve any questions or concerns that came up immediately upon their request; we intended to give this customer white-glove treatment.

We re-packaged and presented our proposal with all of the exceptional services and support we planned to provide. We had one twist: we didn't want to just tell them what we could do, we wanted to show them. This demonstration was not only important to us; it was important to them. Their initiative was to meet a critical need, and the investment was in the millions. The decision was important to them and their executive sponsors. We requested a head-to-head comparison between our company and the competition in a production environment. We presented the proposal to the prospect, and they accepted the challenge.

In the end, we crushed the competition in performance and exceptional services, and we closed an initial seven-figure order from that company, followed by an eight-figure deal later in the year. The story doesn't end there because we took those best practices and applied them to the other prospects in our pipeline. We closed those deals, too, and then, using our exceptional service, we expanded our footprint in those customers as well. Our success didn't stop there. That year, not only did we meet our quota, we exceeded it. What's more, the sales team was flown to Singapore for the worldwide sales conference to be recognized as the company's number-one sales team in the United States that year. Bob once again exceeded his entire area's sales plan.

A takeaway lesson from this experience is that to expand sales, you must build a solid foundation of exceptional customer service and overall customer experience.

Why Exceptional Customer Service Is So Important

- New Voice Media states United States companies are losing $62 billion per year due to poor customer service.[17]

---

[17] " 75 Customer Service Facts, Quotes & Statistics, How Your Business Can Deliver With the Best of the Best," HelpScout, https://www.helpscout.com/75-customer-service-facts-quotes-statistics/.

- Accenture's research shows that in the United States, "the estimated [lifetime] cost of customers switching due to poor service is $1.6 trillion."[18]
- According to an American Express survey, 73 percent of customers stop doing business with a company because they are dissatisfied with customer service, but the company losing the customer thinks only 21 percent leave because of customer service.[19]

Those are three incredibly powerful observations that highlight the cost of poor service. The statistics are overwhelming! With all of your competitors vying for the same business, you must provide exceptional service. Exceptional customer service is absolutely essential to retain and grow your revenue and profit.

Real-World Scenarios

Consider these two companies:

At Company A, the sales rep runs a victory lap after landing a deal, and then, because his quota is huge, he quickly moves on to focus on closing the next big deal. Of course, his sales manager is beating him over the head to close the next deal and make the quarterly number.

Everyone is busy slapping the sales rep on the back, giving him high fives, while the customer is floundering trying to figure out what he has purchased and how it can easily be deployed to meet his business problem. There is no one to be found to help him. The sales rep has moved on. The customer is not happy.

---

[18] "U.S. Companies Losing Customers As Consumers Demand More Human Interaction, Accenture Strategy Study Finds," March 23, 2016, Accenture, https://newsroom.accenture.com/news/us-companies-losing-customers-as-consumers-demand-more-human-interaction-accenture-strategy-study-finds.htm

[19] "75 Customer Service Facts, Quotes & Statistics, How Your Business Can Deliver With the Best of the Best," HelpScout, https://www.helpscout.net/75-customer-service-facts-quotes-statistics/.

Now, consider Company B, where the sales rep stays involved until there is a seamless transition to the post-sales or services team. Sales, along with the extended team, continues to stay involved in the customer's success throughout the life of the relationship. Sales regularly asks how his company can help the customer to be even more successful. The company makes the customer so happy that they want to have Company B help them solve their other problems—thus expanding revenue. Now, the customer is so delighted they want to tell everyone they know how great Company B is, which further expands revenue.

Which company do you think will expand their revenues more quickly? Correct—Company B, the company that doesn't abandon its new customer and continues to develop the relationship and stays involved after the first sale and each subsequent sale.

Exceptional customer service is vital to retain your customers. Providing exceptional customer service can make a significant impact on the overall customer experience.

The customer experience is broader than customer service because it encompasses every interaction with your company.

Customer Experience Is A High-Stakes Requirement

To grow revenue and profit, your company needs to create an exceptional overall customer experience.

- According to Temkin Group, "A moderate increase in customer experience generates an average revenue increase of $823 million over three years for a company with $1 billion in annual revenues."[20]

---

[20] Yifat Mor and Jay Baer, "Why Customer Experience," Convince and Convert, (ConvinceandConvert.com), https://www.convinceandconvert.com/online-customer-experience/why-customer-experience/.

- Gartner found by 2016, "89 percent of the companies it surveyed expect to compete mostly on the basis of customer experience. Just four years [prior], the survey showed that only 36 percent of respondents had that plan."[21]
- Gartner also asserts, "customer experience is the new competitive battlefield."[22]
- Walker recently released a study that stated: "by 2020, customer experience will overtake price and product as the key brand differentiator."[23]

HubSpot defines customer experience (CX) as "the impression you leave with your customer, resulting in how they think of your brand, across every stage of the customer journey. Multiple touchpoints factor into the customer experience, and these touchpoints occur on a cross-functional basis. The two primary touchpoints that create the customer experience are people and product."[24]

Okay, you get the point that delivering an exceptional customer experience is vital to retaining customers; but why

---

21 Sujan Patel, "These 6 Companies Are Boosting Growth by Delighting Customers," *Entrepreneur* (Entrepreneur.com, August 24, 2015), https://www.entrepreneur.com/article/249807#.

22 Jake Sorofman and Ed Thompson, "Customer Experience Is the New Competitive Battlefield," Gartner (Gartner.com, June 4, 2015), https://www.gartner.com/en/documents/3069817/customer-experience-is-the-new-competitive-battlefield.

23 Sean Cotter, "Customer Experience Will Overtake Price and Product," The Chat Shop (Thechatshop.com, February 1, 2019), https://www.thechatshop.com/blog/customer-experience-will-overtake-price-product.

24 Jason Bordeaux, "What is Customer Experience (and Why It's So Important)," HubSpot Blog, https://blog.hubspot.com/service/what-is-customer-experience.

is it so important to expanding sales? Simple: to expand sales, excellent customer service, and the overall customer experience of working with your company, leads customers to trust you, want to work with you, and ultimately buy more of your products, increasing your revenues in the process.

Here is the reality of the difficulty of delivering on the strategy of exceptional customer service: retaining customers isn't easy, much less expanding your footprint into them. To retain your customers, are you going out of your way to ensure a satisfying—not just better but extraordinary—customer experience? If so, you're in the minority. According to the *Harvard Business Review*, "the average American business loses 50 percent of its customers every five years, with two-thirds of them citing inadequate customer care as their primary reason for leaving. Additionally, 91 percent of small businesses do nothing to retain their existing clients."[25]

Consider This Best-Case Scenario

You've landed the contract. You've ensured the order was correct. The order was seamlessly delivered to the customer, and the delivery of your solution was flawless. You provided timely, exceptional onboarding and training so the customer could begin using your solution immediately and ultimately achieve value. Most importantly, you ensured they received the outcomes they purchased your solution for, such as increased revenue, lower cost, better brand recognition, or increased security, to name a few. The net result: flawless execution by your company and maximum value for your customer. And the outcome—the customer is overwhelmed with satisfaction.

---

[25] "The Power of Customer Retention Infographic," Kapow Insider (Kapow.com, March 22, 2013), https://www.kapow.com/blog/event-tips/customer-retention-infographic/.

Reality Check

How often does this scenario occur? In most cases, it's not that easy. It takes a well-orchestrated effort from every department in your company—from engineering great solutions to great sales and operations to outstanding customer support—to deliver an exceptional customer experience.

Perception Is Reality—What You Need To Do

It's no easy endeavor to execute flawlessly, and to do so requires a lot of coordination, process, and perseverance. Regardless of the amount of work it takes, on an ongoing basis, your service needs to be exceptional. What's more, the focus to be exceptional is not just during the initial installation, but during the life of the customer relationship. Every time there's a problem—real or perceived, big or small—that problem must be addressed to achieve an exceptional experience. As you can imagine, during the life of the relationship, every single employee can have a powerful impact on the company's overall results.

In the past, companies signed multi-million-dollar software or hardware solutions, often in the form of a multi-year or perpetual license, with all the revenue being recognized upon installation. Companies felt like they'd hit the motherload. But that was the past, and the new models are often based on SaaS, cloud, or subscription licenses. In many cases, the new license is a monthly subscription. In some cases, the solution is sticky—that is, hard to replace—but in many cases, not so hard. The ability for customers to churn, or move to a competitor's solution, is higher than it's ever been.

This volatility means that your solution has a high probability of being switched out because there are often low switching costs. Every day, you are at risk of losing an extension or renewal of that initial sale. Because of these new models and heightened customer expectations, companies today have to do everything they can to retain and delight their current customers.

As noted, competition is fierce, the subscription model is often unforgiving, solutions are less sticky than they were in the past, and your best chance for survival is to retain your customers and ward off the competition. How? First and foremost, you must go above and beyond to retain your current customers by providing an exceptional customer experience.

The focus on customer experience has grown exponentially in recent years, and for good reason: companies need to focus on delivering an outstanding customer experience if they want to have any chance to succeed in this highly competitive and unforgiving marketplace.

Service Is A Competitive Battleground—Plan To Win

How bad is the lack of service in the marketplace, and why is service a competitive battleground? Is customer dissatisfaction with service really a problem, and if so, just how ugly is it out there? Consider these statistics:

- According to *1st Financial Training Services,* "96 percent of unhappy customers don't complain; however, 91 percent of those will simply leave and never come back."[26]
- A study by American Express 2017 Customer Service Barometer found that "more than half of Americans have scrapped a planned purchase or transaction because of bad service."[27]

---

[26] Colin Shaw, "15 Statistics That Should Change the Business World," Beyond Philosophy (Beyondphilosophy.com, June 10, 2013), https://beyondphilosophy.com/15-statistics-that-should-change-the-business-world-but-havent/.

[27] Help Scout, "75 Customer Service Stats and Facts You Can't Afford to Ignore." https://www.helpscout.com/75-customer-service-facts-quotes-statistics/.

- In "Understanding Customers," Ruby Newell-Legner states, "Twelve positive experiences are necessary to make up for just one unresolved negative one."[28]

Customers today sound pretty fickle. What are you supposed to do, shower them with love? Well, yes . . . if you want to beat out the competition and stay in business.

Okay, okay, enough is enough. These quotations raise many concerns, but here are three additional statistics that should cause you to stand up and pay attention:

- According to *Entrepreneur*, "80 percent of businesses believe they provide 'superior' customer service. But only 8 percent of customers would describe the service they've received in such glowing terms."[29]
- Another source states: "Even if you provide a positive customer experience nine out of ten times, that one time you do not could be fatal."[30]
- In their future of customer experience report, PwC surveyed 15,000 consumers and found that one in three customers will leave a brand they love after just one bad experience, while 92 percent would completely abandon a company after two or three negative interactions.[31]

---

[28] Colin Shaw, "15 Statistics That Should Change the Business World," Beyond Philosophy (Beyondphilosophy.com, June 10, 2013), https://beyondphilosophy.com/15-statistics-that-should-change-the-business-world-but-havent/.

[29] Colleen DeBaise, "Stop Losing Money and Focus on Customer Service (Infographic)," *Entrepreneur*, September 3, 2013, https://www.entrepreneur.com/article/228129.

[30] Toma Kulbyte, "37 Powerful Customer Experience Statistics to Know in 2020," CRM Blog: Articles, Tips and Strategies by SuperOffice, February 26, 2020, https://www.superoffice.com/blog/customer-experience-statistics/.

[31] Toma Kulbyte, "37 Powerful Customer Experience Statistics to Know in 2020."

How To Succeed At Offering An Extraordinary Customer Experience

Here are three top ways to make fast progress when attempting to improve your customers' experience with your company. In this section, we'll cover focusing on feedback, providing superior customer service, and making the customer experience part of your culture.

Focus On Feedback

To provide an exceptional customer experience, focus on customer feedback. It is vital that you ask, respond, and communicate back to customers your commitment to providing them with an exceptional customer experience.

What's important to embrace is some customers feel they are receiving poor support, but companies aren't aware of it. That's why ABPs and QBRs (covered in more detail in Chapter Six) and NPS and CSAT surveys (covered in more detail in Chapter Seven), and ongoing communications are so vital. The key is to request feedback and then, most importantly, do something about it—and let your customers know what you're doing or what you've done.

Providing exceptional customer satisfaction doesn't have to be as hard as it sounds. As you've read, the key is communication. Communicate often with your customers and listen to their feedback. Most importantly, act on the feedback. I've experienced several companies that focus on compensation and rewards to sales reps for getting CSAT surveys filled out. However, I have not seen as many companies compensate or reward sales reps for ensuring the company provides any feedback to the customer regarding the company's actions to address the customer's concerns. Consider how you can provide exceptional service to your customers—just through action and communications!

The key is to measure your success. Adhere to metrics such as NPS and CSAT surveys and consider churn, customer loyalty, customer engagement, customer retention, cost of acquisition, lifetime value (LTV), and other metrics as applicable, but don't go overboard initially. Some companies avoid using metrics because they perceive them as leading to an internal negative focus. You don't have to go overboard, but the goal is for the unified team to focus on continuous improvement of the customer experience. How can you expect to be the best if you are not micro-focused on being exemplary and making continuous improvements to remain a leader?

Provide Superior Customer Service

Customers expect their problems to be solved. They expect them to be resolved expeditiously, but more importantly, correctly. They also have different perspectives on media. Do they want to call you with an issue with a computer or a phone or a mobile device, use social media, text you, email you, or set up an immediate chat session? It is important to know how your customers like to communicate. Customers want their vendors to know their histories, and with that, vendors must consolidate their customers' input into a single repository for quick access to the different mediums used by their customers. In this new market, customers have little tolerance for delayed resolution.

> *"Customers don't expect you to be perfect. They do expect you to fix things when they go wrong."*
> —DONALD PORTER[32]

---

[32] Blake Morgan, "101 Of The Best Customer Experience Quotes", April 3, 2019, Forbes (Forbes.com), https://www.forbes.com/sites/blakemorgan/2019/04/03/101-of-the-best-customer-experience-quotes/#7e6ddc1a45fd.

Make Customer Experience Part Of Your Culture

Who typically takes the call when a customer calls in with a technical question, concern, complaint, or downed system? Technical support? Do you have a customer experience toll-free number or a chat line? These teams may be called the customer experience center, contact center, contact call center, command center, or something similar.

Every employee makes an impression on customers, especially when a customer is dissatisfied with an issue. How customer-friendly and effective are your contact center personnel, onsite or online technicians? You need to make sure everyone is measured on providing an exceptional customer experience. That step is critical toward making a great customer experience a part of your company's culture.

> Tony Hsieh, founder and CEO of Zappos, said: "Customer service shouldn't be a single department; it should be the entire company."[33]

Unfortunately, many customers churn because they started with a problem, whether small or large, and then had a worse experience in trying to resolve their issue. The attempted resolution escalated from bad to worse. Most of us have probably experienced feeling frustrated that a product didn't work—think laptop, phone, or washing machine—calling a hotline, and the person responding did not come across as responsive. This seeming indifference made the matter worse, and it spiraled into overwhelming frustration. The key is we must all put ourselves in our customers' shoes. No matter how frustrated the customer is, or even how unrealistic their concerns may

---

[33] Help Scout, "75 Customer Service Stats and Facts You Can't Afford to Ignore." https://www.helpscout.com/75-customer-service-facts-quotes-statistics/.

feel, customer perception is our reality, and we need to deliver an outstanding experience every time. Just one lost customer can result in a significant hit to the top and bottom line.

The customer service department is important, but it doesn't end there. Your entire organization needs to be customer centric. Let's move to sales next.

Set Up A Customer-Centric Organization

There are many ways to set up a customer-centric organization. The key is providing the right resources to offer the best level of service for your customers' needs. In this section, we'll cover hunters and farmers, Major Account Managers (MAMs) and Customer Success Teams (CSTs).

Hunters And Farmers

You've probably heard the make-up of a sales team, including hunters and farmers. Let's start with hunters who find new business. Some companies refer to them as big whale hunters, elephant hunters, dragon slayers, big game hunters, along with other similar names. They are called "hunters" because they are a special type of sales rep who loves to go after big game or hunt new accounts. Often, after that sales rep has slayed the dragon, their quota drives them to go slay the next dragon. This momentum is great for new business, but it doesn't ensure your new customer's outcomes and long-term satisfaction are the first priority.

Some companies put farmers in place. Farmers work with the existing customer base to ensure their delight and provide new solutions and upgrades. Many larger companies add MAMs to focus on supporting their largest accounts. In the more recent sales go-to-market (GTM) models, you often see an enhancement in the form of CSTs, who also focus on delivering exceptional customer experiences and driving incremental business in existing accounts.

Let's dig a little deeper into these two areas.

Major Account Managers

Farmers on large strategic accounts may be called MAMs, global account managers, or even select major account managers. They are put in place, particularly at larger companies, for a select number of the largest accounts. Some of their quotas are enormous. I've seen $1 billion quotas and more; often, very senior executives hold these roles. They typically own the strategic account plan, and they are often accountable for orchestrating all relationships, communications, and all sales into those very large accounts. Major account teams are often matrixed and include a wide breadth of resources to ensure these customers are provided the best support.

Customer Success Teams

You have probably heard a lot of buzz about CSTs or Customer Support or Customer Success Managers (CSMs). Thus, I'll spend more time on the CSM's role in delivering an exceptional customer experience.

As mentioned previously, in many companies, the sales rep closes a deal, but then moves on to the next deal to meet his or her quota. The CSM is then assigned to the account to provide post-sales support and to stay actively engaged with the customer throughout the relationship. The CSM's role is to focus on retaining and delighting the customer after the initial sale is made.

Because of the vital nature of retaining customers and ensuring predictable deferred revenue streams, particularly in a SaaS model, more and more companies of all sizes are adding

CSMs, often as part of a CST. These teams are responsible for maintaining an ongoing relationship with customers to ensure the company is meeting its service requirements and Service Level Agreements (SLAs), ensuring satisfied customers. CSMs may be involved with customers' onboarding as well as their day-to-day activities to help them drive best practices, helping them determine what's working and what's not, thus enabling the customer to get the greatest value out of their solution. In some cases, CSMs are responsible for renewals, upgrades, upselling, and cross-selling.

I have seen CSTs report to services, operations, or sales organizations. When CSTs are in the sales organization, companies may assign a sales quota aligned with the customers the CSM supports. Many companies, however, don't give quotas to the CSMs, feeling that doing so may put more focus on meeting a sales quota over providing exceptional service. You'll have to decide, based on your circumstances, what would deliver the best results for your company.

CSMs focus on building lasting and consultative relationships with customer accounts. They concentrate on helping customers achieve their business outcomes. They focus on customer feedback, including through either NPS or CSAT surveys or both (covered in Chapter Seven), as well as leading or being involved in ABPs and QBRs (covered in Chapter Six). The roles that might be associated with members of the CST include those in the graphic below:

CSMs can also assist with delivering the messaging that is vital to your customers, such as new offers, which we will cover in Chapter Five: Promotions and Programs.

Assess And Quantify Customer Success Metrics

Amity created the following test to assess the maturity of your customer success. It is a great test that only requires a few minutes to take and will help you determine where there are gaps that you potentially need to fill or prioritize:

1. Do you have an up-to-date list of all your customers?
2. Do you measure churn and the impact it has on your company's growth?
3. Do you segment your customer base?
4. Do you track product and feature adoption?
5. Do you know the health of all of your customers?
6. Do you have a documented onboarding process?
7. Do you know the renewal date of all your customers?
8. Do you know how your customer is using your product?

9. Do you know when you last engaged with your customer?
10. Do you measure team performance?
11. Do you communicate how much revenue is at risk?
12. Do you measure the impact your CST is having?
13. Do you measure the value being gained by your customer?
14. Do you have a success plan for each customer (or tier)?
15. Do you regularly report Customer Success KPIs?
16. Do you measure and track the cost of retention?[34]

Real-Life Experience

I have worked in several companies that had incredibly strong customer success teams. The teams focused on ensuring that we met our customers' expectations, from SLAs to outcomes, to key performance indicators, to total cost of ownership objectives, to return on investment objectives. In addition to ensuring successful onboarding, they ensured the customer was supported throughout the relationship. The members of the CSTs were assigned to specific accounts and were responsible for ensuring their customers' ongoing satisfaction.

Additionally, the CSTs conducted regular reviews with the customer to ensure we received regular and frequent feedback on how we were performing. CSTs were responsible for communicating their feedback throughout the company, so that all owners across all divisions, departments, and functional areas were accountable for addressing any issues. The CSMs were the glue that held the sales teams, engineering, product management, marketing, finance, engineering, and other departments in lockstep. They truly focused on the

---

[34] Matthew McLaren, "The Amity Test: 16 Steps to Better Customer Success," Amity, February 16, 2020, http://customer-success.getamity.com/amity-blog/the-amity-test-16-steps-to-better-customer-success.

voice of the customer and ensured the rest of the organization responded to the customer's needs in a timely fashion.

According to Qualtrics, the voice of the customer "describes your customer's feedback about their experiences with and expectations for your products or services. It focuses on customer needs, expectations, understandings, and product improvement."[35]

With regular discussions, feedback, resolution, and ongoing customer satisfaction ratings, we kept a close pulse on how we were meeting customer expectations. In many cases, CSMs were the most common face to the customer. Behind the scenes, we had an incredible team of sales, technical, engineering, product, marketing, operational, finance, and others who were all involved in ensuring execution against the customer's requirements. My experience with CSTs aligned tightly cross-functionally resulted in a swift increase in providing an exceptional customer experience and, on one team, achieving a four-fold increase in revenues over a two-year period.

Summary

Providing exceptional customer service and overall customer experience is the foundation of a successful business and the best route to increased revenue and profit. According to one source: "89 percent of companies see customer experience as a key factor in driving customer loyalty and retention."[36]

---

[35] "What is Voice of The Customer (VoC)?," https://www.qualtrics.com/experience-management/customer/what-is-voice-of-customer/.

[36] Khalid Saleh, "Customer Acquisition Vs. Retention Costs – Statistics And Trends." See sources on this link https://www.invespcro.com/blog/customer-acquisition-retention/.

To further emphasize the importance of providing an exceptional customer experience, the Temkin Group states, "73 percent of companies with 'above average' customer experience maturity perform better financially than their competitors."[37]

You must satisfy your customers and ensure that they have a positive impression of your company and a positive experience with your company. Poor perceptions impact other prospects: almost certainly, those customers impacted by poor performance won't buy from your company again, or refer you positively, unless they experience a significantly more positive experience.

To deliver extraordinary customer service, take into account:

- Churn rates are higher than they've ever been; the customer's perception is reality, not yours.
- Service is a competitive battleground, and you must focus on this area if you plan to grow, much less survive.

Win by:

- Focusing on feedback
- Providing exceptional customer service
- Making customer experience a part of your culture
- Setting up a customer-centric organization
- Assessing and quantifying customer success team metrics

The next chapter focuses on the "X" strategy of the Land and EXPAND Sales Framework—e**X**pansion Revenue with Upsell and Cross-Sell. Once you've provided exceptional customer service and overall customer experience, you are in a position to expand your market share within that account. Upselling

[37] Help Scout, "75 Customer Service Stats and Facts You Can't Afford to Ignore." https://www.helpscout.com/75-customer-service-facts-quotes-statistics/.

and cross-selling provide incremental solutions to your existing customers and expands revenue and profit for your company.

CHAPTER 4

X Is For EXpansion Revenue With Upsell And Cross-Sell

"On average, loyal customers are worth up to ten times as much as their first purchase."[38]
—White House Office of Consumer Affairs

Another strategy of the Land and EXPAND Sales Framework is X—eXpansion Revenue with cross-selling and upselling. Cross-selling is a complementary offer, such as "Would you like fries with that order?" Upselling is an upgrade offer, such as "Would you like a double patty burger versus the single patty?" If you don't tell your customers what products and services you have to sell them, how will they know?

Journey To Success

This particular company was a successful Fortune 100 company that sold what was called on-premise solutions, including data centers. Basically, that meant it offered hardware and software solutions located at the customer site. It had a loyal customer base. There were three regions in

---

[38] James Macquire, "Customer Loyalty: Using Data to Keep the Love Alive", Experian, June 5, 2018, https://www.experian.com/blogs/insights/2018/06/customer-loyalty-using-data-to-keep-the-love-alive/.

North America, and one of the regions had a quota of over $500 million in sales. Unfortunately, that region had missed their quota the prior year. Nancy, the new sales leader of North America, had a successful career at this company, with many high-visibility promotions. She had just taken on the new role and saw this position as an exceptional opportunity to advance her already successful career. She decided to adjust the leadership of the three regions and reached out to me to run one of them.

The advent of "cloud" solutions had come onto the market. Our company was early to market in offering a cloud solution, but many of our sales reps across the company were reticent about being first to market. Our on-premises solutions worked, so why confuse our customers? At first, many customers were apprehensive about putting their sacred data in the cloud. Many sales reps decided to ignore talking about cloud-based data storage with customers. Why disrupt the company's current revenue stream?

The competition and buzz in the marketplace about moving to the cloud were relentless. Most of my colleagues continued to take the stance to wait and see. But if we weren't telling our customers about our cloud solutions, our competitors were. My regional team decided to take the bull by the horns. Again, if we weren't talking about the cloud, our competition was, and we were not willing to provide even a crack for our competitors to wedge themselves into our accounts.

My team focused on educating our customers about the company's new cloud offerings. We were transparent in telling them, before our competition beat us to the punch, that we offered these new solutions. We also summarized what the industry publications were saying, both pros and cons. Other teams were concerned that they might confuse the customer and open up their customer's pursuit of looking at options. But if our sales team didn't tell them that our company had options, our customers wouldn't know, and they might leave us out of their cloud platform evaluations.

My team made the decision to position ourselves as offering flexible options. We decided to offer a full suite of options. We showed our customers that our company was forward-thinking and that we were committed to both options, on-premise and cloud, and when they were ready to transition, we'd be there to help them move seamlessly to the new cloud platforms.

Even though in the first year, most of our customers stayed with their on-premises solutions where they already felt comfortable, they became confident we could take them into the future when they were ready.

Even though cloud adoption was slow initially, we maintained a higher rate of retention of our current customers than our peers, we continued to upgrade and expand the customer's current on-premise solutions, and we sold a record number of new cloud solutions.

Our expansion strategy paid off. That year, we exceeded the quota plan of over $500 million and achieved almost $900 million in orders. Working together, Nancy, I, and the entire team were successful in exceeding expectations.

Takeaway: upsell and cross-sell EXPANDs sales.

There is an enormously rich opportunity to be had when you view your customers strategically, understand their business, and address as many of their needs as possible. The first step is to build a foundation of exceptional customer service and overall customer experience. Once you have built that foundation, you are in a position to upsell and cross-sell your other solutions more strategically, leading to significantly more revenue and profit.

Real-World Scenarios

Consider these two scenarios.

Your customer is dissatisfied with the outcomes of their last purchase with your company. The solution didn't meet their needs in the way they expected, and they could never get anyone to address their problems. They feel they had been sold a bill of goods and when they called technical support to get assistance, they were told the features sold weren't in the manual the support team member was looking at and the employee who knew how to implement that variation of the solution had left the company. The customer then tried to call the sales rep on numerous occasions, but the sales rep had moved to a new part of the company and didn't return any of their calls. The customer then tried the sales rep's manager, but she didn't return any calls either. After numerous calls, the customer became frustrated and not only questioned the viability of the solution but the commitment of the company.

Think this customer will be interested in any of your company's new offers? Probably not.

Consider a different company and a different customer. This customer is proactively introduced to your pre-sales team, which works with them to verify the solution will work in their environment. The customer's technical resources team is introduced to your technical resources staff so that your team can be available to answer any questions and to develop a one-to-one relationship. The customer's technical team and yours discuss, in technical depth, how your solution will meet the customer's expectations. After the implementation, if the pre-sales technical person isn't available, you provide a chat and phone support line available 24/7 and focus on expeditious resolution of all issues and questions. You make a list of contacts with phone numbers and emails, so they always have a resource to contact, or if they need to escalate a situation.

You and your team closely monitor the implementation's success, with regular check-ins to ensure your company is tracking the customer's defined expectations. Once you've met your customer's goals, you don't stop communicating with them. Your company regularly checks in to make sure the customer achieves the outcomes they expect. You share with the customer other best practices of companies like theirs so they can continue to get more benefits out of the solution that they acquired from you. You offer training and webinars that they can use within their own department or forward to others in their company, such as other departments which might be interested.

Do you think the second company might be interested in any of your new offers? Absolutely! Expansion revenue through upselling and cross-selling begins with a satisfied customer.

Expansion Through Upsell And Cross-Sell

First things first, what are your customers buying today? All of your products? The lowest-priced solutions or the top of your offerings? Do they have your solutions in one location, or have they deployed them globally? Are your solutions in one functional area or many? A great way to look at this issue holistically is to create a white space analysis.

Wave6 Insights defines white space as "the gap between what products or services your customer has invested in and the other products or services that your company or business has to offer."[39]

You need to determine what other solutions will potentially benefit each customer. Identify your customer's preferences and prior purchase history. Doing this analysis by customer allows you to target your offers better, instead of making a widespread blast that doesn't yield great results and doesn't show your customers that you understand their individual business. Determine what solutions your company offers that would benefit or enhance their specific needs. This is your opportunity to upsell or cross-sell your solutions. I'll come back to the white space analysis later in this chapter.

What do the terms "upsell" and "cross-sell" mean, and what is the difference between those two terms? In the example below, cross-selling means to offer a solution that is complementary (fries) but different from the original request (burger). Upselling, on the other hand, means to offer a solution that is an upgrade (double-patty hamburger) over the original request (single-patty hamburger).

---

[39] Wave6 Blog Team, "How to Use White Space Analysis to Sell More to Existing Customers," Wave6 (Emtec, April 26, 2016), http://explore.wave6.com/blog/how-to-use-white-space-analysis-to-sell-more-to-existing-customers.

Expand Revenue Through Upselling

One source defines upselling as "the practice of encouraging customers to purchase a comparable higher-end product than the one in question, while cross-selling invites customers to buy related or complementary items.... Upselling and cross-selling are mutually beneficial when done properly, providing maximum value to customers, and increasing revenue."[40]

The aforementioned source also states: "Upselling often employs comparison charts to market higher-end products to customers. Showing [them] that other versions or models may better fulfill their needs can increase AOV [(Average Order Value)] and help users walk away more satisfied with their purchase."[41]

Consider the example of offering the bronze, silver, gold, and platinum versions of a product. The customer knows whether they are buying at the low end or the high end. They are aware through your marketing messaging that there are

[40] "What's the Difference between Upselling & Cross-Selling? [2018]," BigCommerce, March 4, 2020, https://www.bigcommerce.com/ecommerce-answers/what-difference-be-tween-upselling-and-cross-selling/.

[41] "What's the Difference between Upselling & Cross-Selling?", 2018.

different tiers of solutions or services. They may, in fact, want to start at the base level and then upgrade only if needed or as they gain more trust in you as a vendor. By making the customer aware of the upgrade opportunities, you are upselling the higher levels of offers.

Let's go back to a term mentioned previously—AOV. What exactly is AOV? AOV equals the sum of revenue generated divided by the number of orders taken. The value of increasing your AOV is that your pipeline value will go up, your average transaction size will go up, and you will achieve your quota, revenue, or booking targets more quickly. Net, increasing your AOV, is a key component to growing the revenue of your company. How do you improve your AOV? By upselling. When was the last time you went through a drive-thru window, and the restaurant employee asked if you would like to upgrade that medium soft drink to a large one for only ten cents more? Or would you like to upgrade from six nuggets to twelve? When you bought your most recent new car, did the salesperson suggest the luxury version with a better stereo system, GPS, leather seats, or fancier sporty tires? What about the airline who asks if you would like more legroom at an additional fee? Or how about business class or first class? They are all upsells to the current solution you have expressed an interest in purchasing.

Let's say you sell a software solution. Do you have new features that can be added to your customer's existing platform for a great price during the solution's initial release? Or do you have a new, enhanced version of your software with a lot of innovative, best-in-class features, and you offer early adopters an exceptional early bird special? Do you offer tiered, incremental levels of service? That's upselling.

You can also increase your revenue through cross-selling.

Expand Revenue Through Cross-Selling

According to the same source mentioned above, "Cross-selling identifies products that satisfy additional, complementary needs that are unfulfilled by the original item. For example, a comb could be cross sold to a customer purchasing a blow dryer. Oftentimes, cross-selling points users to products they would have purchased anyway; by showing them at the right time, a store ensures they make the sale."[42]

To increase your revenue, you might bundle related merchandise. The last time you shopped on Amazon, you probably noted: "Customers Who Bought This Item Also Bought…" or "Frequently Bought Together." Amazon does a great job at cross-selling. In 2015, *Forbes* noted, at the time, Amazon generated more than 35 percent of its revenue through cross-selling activities![43]

At the checkout stand, do you find yourself looking at the magazines or candies? You hadn't planned to purchase them, but they are placed at the checkout stand to spark your interest and potentially increase the store's revenue. When you spoke to your insurance agent about your car insurance, did they mention adding your home insurance to get a better rate? This is cross-selling. These examples demonstrate complementary opportunities to increase your revenue.

In your business, think about what solutions you have that can be tiered—bronze, silver, gold, and platinum, thus, upsell. Think about what solutions you can bundle together that complement each other, thus, cross-sell.

---

[42] "What's the Difference between Upselling & Cross-Selling?" 2018.

[43] Chuck Cohn, "A Beginner's Guide To Upselling And Cross-Selling," Forbes (*Forbes* Magazine, May 15, 2015), https://www.forbes.com/sites/chuckcohn/2015/05/15/a-beginners-guide-to-upselling-and-cross-selling/#407af3f52912.

The lines between upselling and cross-selling can get blurred. This haziness is not something to be concerned with. What matters is that you are offering an incremental solution of interest to your customer and, at the same time, increasing your company's revenue.

There is a time and a place for upselling and cross-selling. Personally, I'm not happy when I call the credit card company with a problem or question, and before they let me hang up, they want to upgrade my credit card to the new fancy version with all the bells and whistles for only $450. Or when I place a call to my mobile phone provider to determine why I am having an issue, and they close the call by trying to sell me a new phone. Spending the time to understand your customer and what their perceived needs might be, or how they might leverage the up-and-coming trends in your industry that might interest them, goes a long way, versus an un-targeted blast. Offering upsell or cross-sell solutions that don't tie in any way to the customer can, on the other hand, tarnish your credibility.

White Space Analysis To Target New Opportunities

Let's discuss when it is the right time to upsell and cross-sell. First, you need to conduct a white space analysis. Below is a basic example of a white space analysis for an individual account.

WHITE SPACE Analysis					
Solution/ Description/ Outcomes	Currently Installed/ Dept/Loc	Not Installed/ Dept/Loc	Defined Need Yes/No	AOV	Opportunity/Strategy to Offer

Fill in one chart for each customer based on what products they have purchased or installed today. What is not purchased is white space. In that white space, is there potential in other departments, and other locations, and if so, what is the average order value? What is the strategy to penetrate the account for that product offering? Of course, this chart offers a quick snapshot, but that's what you are initially looking for, an overview of the opportunities you have in each account.

Uncover Opportunities Through Communications

Communicating with your customers is key to uncovering sales opportunities. Both sales and marketing play an important role here. In the current selling models, and with the advent of the internet, digital and content marketing, as well as social media, marketing is more important than ever before.

According to a recent survey by Gartner, "57 percent of the typical business-to-business customer's decision-making process is complete before the customer even contacts a potential supplier."[44] Forbes.com reports some respondents

---

[44] "The Challenger Sale, Compete and win in a customer-empowered world," Gartner, https://www.gartner.com/en/salesservice/insights/challenger-sale.

reported being over 70 percent complete in their decision making before reaching out to potential suppliers.[45]

Even if the customer has already bought one or more of your company's products, marketing still plays an important role. Even though both your sales reps and CSTs have a direct line to the customer, they can't reach everyone about everything. In this case, marketing helps to package up the cross-sell and upsell messaging proactively and professionally and helps the sales reps and CSTs deliver the message in a targeted way. Since the sales rep and CSTs have established a relationship, and they are building trusted advisor status with your customers, their delivery of a packaged solution will typically have a higher close rate. In this case, both marketing and sales hold important symbiotic roles. Revenue is impacted in a positive way by leveraging sales and marketing resources to sell to existing customers.

Increasing your sales may be as simple as expanding your solution beyond the current installation to other locations, other departments, or other subsidiaries within your existing accounts.

Let's go back to the white space analysis. You've mapped each of your accounts and which of your company's products they use. What solutions have they not purchased, and at what value? Beyond upselling and cross-selling current customers, have you deployed your company's solutions department-wide, division-wide, or company-wide?

The key is to understand the customer's business and how your solutions could help them solve an existing or potential dilemma. Define the problem statement, the issue your solution

---

[45] Ryan Erskine, "How To Turn B2B Buyers Into Sales Leads, According To Data," *Forbes*, Dec. 28, 2017, https://www.forbes.com/sites/ryanerskine/2017/12/28/how-to-turn-b2b-buyers-into-sales-leads-according-to-data/#5c4072045a18.

solves, and the outcomes that your solution provides. The white space analysis uncovers opportunities for upselling and cross-selling across the customer's entire organization. The key to upselling and cross-selling is understanding the customer's business and how your solutions help them solve problems.

Assess The Competition To Win

Once you define the gaps, also assess the competition. What are the strengths, weaknesses, opportunities, and threats (SWOT) of the competition? When you understand your competition, you can determine which areas of white space are the areas where you have the greatest opportunity to beat or displace the competition. Consider the value of each opportunity, where you have the best fit to provide your customer with additional value, and where you have the highest probability of success.

COMPETITION/SWOT				
Competitor	Strengths	Weaknesses	Opportunities	Threats
Competitor #1				
Competitor #2				
Competitor #3				
Competitor #4				
Competitor #5				
Assess Yourself				
Unique Differentiation				

What areas might you measure to assess your customer's perception of your company? Consider your strength in areas such as your relationships—are you aligned with the decision-makers, with the right relationships from your company? What is your perceived value, both from a company and a product perspective, as seen by the customer? What is your balance of trade (BOT)? BOT is the amount you purchase from the customer compared to how much they buy from you. Some companies use the BOT metric as an opportunity to upsell and cross-sell.

Increase Opportunities Through ABPs, QBRs, NPS, And CSAT Surveys

In addition to the initial white space analysis, see Chapter Six on Account Business Plans (ABPs) and Quarterly Business Plans (QBRs) to understand your customer's needs better and to discern more clearly what upsell and cross-sell opportunities will meet their objectives. What are the results of your Net Promoter Score (NPS) and customer satisfaction (CSAT) surveys at the account? See Chapter Seven on NPS and CSAT surveys to determine the level of satisfaction with your accounts and what needs to be addressed to satisfy your customers and in what incremental solutions they might be interested. These additional activities will provide incremental upsell and cross-sell opportunities.

Be sure not to bombard your customer with too many upsell and cross-sell opportunities. You will not only frustrate your customers; you may look desperate. Make your company's messaging relevant to their needs.

As noted in the prior chapter, but worth repeating, to ensure you have the ability to upsell and cross-sell, first make sure you are providing an exceptional customer experience. Once you are delivering an exceptional customer experience, you will have a customer who is receptive to your upsell and cross-sell strategies.

Real-Life Experience

In one company, we offered data marts, typically purchased by a department, and also due to the solution's comparatively smaller size, a great way to establish the first sale and prove our products' value. Then, as the customer leveraged the solution and benefited from its powerful capabilities, we expanded into other departments and used the initial department as a reference. Additionally, those data marts had the potential to expand to data warehouses, which were significantly larger in scope.

Another strategy that we implemented was related to cross-selling the enterprise resource planning, supply chain, and customer relationship management software solutions that we offered, which were popular among the many other offers that we provided. We ensured that we understood the customer's needs, and we communicated the applicable offers in our solution suite. The customer might start with one software solution and then expand into our other solutions as their needs expanded. Many customers found our solutions were a better fit than their current vendor, and they ultimately switched from that vendor's solution to ours. In addition, we had an initiative to help our customers consolidate the number of vendors they worked with. We had a program to incentivize our customers to select us for several of their solutions. As their needs expanded, we offered bundled pricing where they could buy more from us and receive a bigger discount. Through ongoing communications and understanding their needs, we developed several qualified upsell and cross-sell opportunities. Ultimately, we far exceeded our order quota objectives on a regular basis.

Summary

There are several ways to create eXpansion revenue:

- Conduct a white space analysis to target new opportunities
- Increase revenue through upselling
- Increase revenue through cross-selling
- Uncover opportunities through communications
- Assess the competition to win
- Increase opportunities through ABPs, QBRs, NPS, and CSAT surveys

The next chapter focuses on the "P" strategy of the Land and EXPAND Sales Framework: **P**romotions and Programs. How can you communicate and package cross-sell and upsell opportunities to existing customers?

CHAPTER 5

P Is For Promotions And Programs

"Without promotion, something terrible happens ... nothing."[46]
—P. T. Barnum

How do your customers know what other services you offer if you don't tell them? In this chapter, we'll focus on three areas: how to broadcast your solutions, offer compelling promotions, and uniquely differentiate your company with innovative programs. These three strategies are intended to gain visibility for your offerings so that they attract attention and stand out in a crowded market.

Journey To Success

A company I worked for had both online transaction processing and data warehouse solutions. Their executives believed the company had a tremendous opportunity to expand sales by combining their solutions with a major data management software company's solutions. The head of the division, Garry, committed to the executive team that he would deliver the results projected. Garry had a phenomenal track record of exceeding every goal he ever set.

---

[46] https://www.brainyquote.com/quotes/p_t_barnum_539959

The annual plan had the company projected to grow significantly faster than their competition, but to sustain that growth, they needed to expand their product portfolio to enlarge their market. Teaming up with an alliance partner would accomplish that goal, but which potential partnership would make the best match?

The company worked with a number of partners that provided complementary solutions that enhanced their offer by making the two combined solutions a more complete and robust offer. The goal, however, was to find the one alliance partner with whom they could jointly go to market, who would bring a unique solution to market, and who would be willing to make a significant investment in the partnership.

Garry asked me to assist with the assessment of the top prospective partners. After an extensive appraisal, we came up with one alliance partner who we were confident would help our company to differentiate itself uniquely in the marketplace. Garry asked me to work with him to develop the programs and promotions—cross-functionally and globally—and to launch this new partnership.

In this role, we worked with our strategic planning department to analyze areas of opportunity to fit the partner into the strategic direction of our company. We worked with marketing to develop programs and promotions that leveraged the strengths of both companies, and we worked with services and engineering to define our unique offer in the marketplace.

We worked closely with the alliance partner to come up with a joint go-to-market plan that included joint sales, joint marketing, and joint engineering. This plan was a lofty endeavor. We planned to build six competency centers around the world and a professional services practice dedicated to this partner's software solutions with plans to grow the practice to one hundred consultants worldwide. Our promotions included a proof of concept (POC) where the customers could try and test our solutions together in the competency centers.

After months of joint planning cross-functionally, we were ready. The rollout of our compelling and innovative program and promotion consisted of a global launch, including a joint press release, messaging blitzes, videos, and world-class events; an abundance of compelling internal and external sales tools such as brochures, case studies, and benchmark reports; and extensive training for sales, support, services, and customers.

In the first year, we achieved over $250 million in joint sales. It was a huge win-win for both companies. Both my company and our new alliance partner benefited by selling more of our technologies together. In partnering together with Garry, and the teams from both companies, we succeeded in exceeding expectations.

Takeaway: programs and promotions deliver incremental revenue and profit.

Real-World Scenarios

Consider these two companies:

Company A has great solutions, and they publish all of them on their website. They put their solutions on brochures, and they build dozens of PowerPoint slide decks. The inside sales group waits patiently by the phone, waiting for it to ring. The outside sales teams are impatiently waiting for the marketing department to bury them with hot leads so they can email those exciting brochures and show up at the customer site and read, word-for-word, every last sentence of their colorful PowerPoint slides. They wait and they wait. The customers have no idea what the company offers because there have been zero outbound communications to them of anything new, and they aren't surfing the company's website in their spare time.

Company B knows the market is crowded, and every company is vying for a piece of the airwaves. They have a team that focuses on creating awareness, leveraging such airwaves as social media, including LinkedIn and Facebook. They offer webinars with industry analysts and other industry leaders. They are active in outreach or push marketing (pushing out their messaging) versus pull marketing (waiting for the customers to come to them). Company B sends out email messaging and content marketing; they also promote themselves in industry publications, both online and in print, as well as at industry events. They know, due to all the noise in the marketplace, they need to create compelling events to get busy customers' attention. They offer creative, compelling promotions that have end dates to create a sense of urgency to buy now. They also have a lot of competition, so they offer a loyalty program that encourages loyal incremental purchases. They also offer a lead referral program with additional discounts and promotions on their solutions.

Which company do you think will expand their sales first? Correct—the second one, Company B, which is active with outbound marketing, pushing out or broadcasting their messaging, and creating compelling promotions.

Let's start with broadcasting your solutions.

Broadcast Your Solutions

Are your customers aware of what you have to offer? Are you communicating your suite of solutions to your customers? If so, how do you broadcast your solutions to your prospective customers? What are the best ways to broadcast your message?

Effective messaging comes first. Do you have a clear, concise, and compelling message?

Create Compelling External Sales Tools

What external sales tools, ones to share with customers, do you have? Below are a few examples. It is important to ensure all of your communications and messaging are consistently aligned.

EXTERNAL SALES TOOLS		
Sales Tools	Names of Tools	URLs
Company Brochures		
Product and Solution		
Data Sheets		
Customer Testimonials		
Case Studies		
Whitepapers		
Presentations		
Websites		
Newsletters		
Videos		
Webinars		
Other		

Brag On Proof Points

In addition to key external messaging, including those mentioned in the graphic above, incorporating external proof points are incredibly helpful in communicating the value that you bring in solving problems. External proof points might include:

- Recognition from analysts, such as accolades from Gartner, Forrester, Frost & Sullivan, Forbes, and others
- Technology awards and top product awards such as Product of the Year, Excellence Award, and Best Practices Award

- Awards highlighting the integrity or innovativeness of your company, such as Best in Innovation Awards, Best in Show Awards, and Top Companies to Work For
- Customer references
- Customer testimonials and quotes
- Case studies and use cases

Leverage Multiple Communications Vehicles

What are some of the communication vehicles you might use to promote your messages?

COMMUNICATIONS			
Vehicles to Communicate	Definition	In Place Y/N	Date to Implement
Website			
Webinars			
Newsletters			
E-Mail Campaigns			
YouTube			
Blogs			
Advertising			
Social Media			
Other			

Create Compelling Internal Sales Tools

Which of your marketing messages are repeatable and resonate well with customers? Do you have an elevator pitch? Battle card? Email scripts? Voicemail scripts? Do you have case studies or success stories? What internal tools do you have for your direct and indirect (channel and alliance partner) sales teams to leverage to aid them in delivering your best and most compelling messaging to customers? It is equally important to make these consistent messages easily available for your customer-facing employees, as well as your channel and alliance partners. Having an online sales portal with the best-of-the-best sales tools is a best practice in providing your sales staff with the tools they need.

INTERNAL SALES TOOLS		
Sales Tools	Names of Tools	URLs
Elevator Pitch		
Success Stories		
Battle Cards		
Qualifying Questions		
Sales Playbooks		
Sales Scripts for Email and Voicemail		
Use Cases		
Competitive Analysis		
SWOT Analysis		
Other		

You want to leverage your success. Your approach should be applied to your customers' other divisions and departments, as well as in a similar industry, if available, with a problem similar to the one you have already solved. It is key to have the case studies and references to validate your success in solving those problems. Of course, you need to ask those customers if they are willing to let you use their name and/or their logo as a customer. Better than that, see if you can write a case study about the problem you solved for them, make a video, and ask for a quote that you can place in use cases, proposals, PowerPoint presentations, or any other format. Use those proof points when you market to other departments within your target company and make those assets available on your website, social media, and other channels.

All of these content pieces that I just mentioned are tools to broadcast your solution to the universe of potential customers. Those pieces provide the message, the content, and the points you want to communicate.

Now we'll move on to cover two additional strategies that create awareness of your offers: promotions and programs.

What Is The Difference Between A Promotion And A Program?

For the purposes of this chapter, consider a promotion an offer that is valid for only a limited time. When you think of programs, envision a structured procedure that is more formal, well-documented, and on-going. Think of programs as typically programmatic, with a set of specific activities or events, and longer lasting than a short-term promotion. In some cases, promotions and programs can be interchangeable. Don't let that nuance bog you down: the key concept is that both promotions and programs provide systematic ways to upsell and cross-sell your solutions.

Offer Persuasive Promotions

Let's start with promotions. What kind of promotions might you consider to EXPAND your market share within your customer base?

Keep in mind that promotions do not translate to "discounting"—the promotion can be as basic as awareness of the solutions you offer and the problems you solve.

Maybe creating awareness and preference is as easy as distributing a monthly or quarterly newsletter or newsflash that highlights a certain solution. Since you've already landed and delighted these customers, you need to let them know what additional products you offer that can help them solve a business problem.

You've probably been the recipient of the promotions cable or internet providers offer, such as specially priced bundles or trade-in promotions to keep customers tied to new contracts that ensure their retention for at least the term of the contract. When that promotion expires, there's often another promotion the provider offers to make certain their customers remain captive. Offering bundles and price promotions are effective upsell and cross-sell opportunities to keep your customer consistently reminded of your solutions.

Below is a list of some examples of promotions that you might consider:

- **Try It/Buy It Promotions**: With this type of promotion, you are offering your customer the ability to try your solution before purchasing it. You want to have a relatively easy implementation, where the customer can try your solution with minimal capital and human resources required to test the solution. It is important that your promotion has clear deliverables so the customer can quickly see the value your solution brings. Creating replicable success criteria that your solution excels at is a key method to ensure your solution comes out on top. Make sure your customers receive excellent support during this try-and-buy period to ensure nothing goes awry, and they are compelled to move forward with a purchase.

- **Free Trials Or Fremiums**: You might consider offering a free limited-feature solution or fremium—that is, a pricing strategy where a product (typically software) or service is provided at no charge. There is a charge for additional features or services. The fremium offer creates awareness for the upgraded solution. The benefit of a fremium is your customer can receive value from your solution while you benefit from the incremental revenues if they decide to upgrade later for the fully featured solution. You might also offer a special promotion to upgrade to the fully featured solution by a certain date.

- **Holiday Promotions**: Holidays are especially important for retailers. For example, your potential customer might need extra compute power to support Black Friday and Cyber Monday transaction levels. Extra compute power might be needed because of all the transactions occurring over the holidays. Black Friday and Cyber Monday create an opportunity to establish a promotion for computing power at a special price to take advantage of that compelling event. In addition, holiday promotions are great for consumers. End-of-year promotions also create a compelling way to assist corporate customers in spending unused budgetary funds before they expire at the end of the fiscal year.

What is a compelling event in sales? A compelling event drives a decision by a certain date, such as an expiring contract, an internally defined date to make a new purchase, new legislation, or a budget about to expire. Time-based promotions run by a company are not as compelling as events driven by your customers, such as purchases they have the budget to buy. However, your company's compelling event can drive a call-to-action and increase sales in a period by providing a time stamp on a special offer that is not planned but is nonetheless a good buy. Having a compelling event goes a long way in accelerating close dates.

- **Trade-In Promotions**: This type of promotion offers a trade-in for older solutions to the latest version. Trade-ins are a great way to upgrade your base and also to remove some of the concerns of life-cycle management as solutions age.

- **Price Match Promise**: Price match guarantees offer to meet the price of any competitor. Best Buy and Walmart are two examples of retailers that offer this type of promotion. This promotion helps drive the customer to a faster, more confident sale.

- **Free Shipping and Free Returns**: Not tacking on additional shipping fees, and making purchases easy to exchange or return, provide a positive customer experience and lower the risk in their purchase decision. You may also require a minimum purchase to receive free shipping, which is another way to increase sales.

- **Bundle Promotions**: You might consider bundling two or more of your offers that complement each other at a lower price point than selling them separately, creating an incentive for the customer to buy more.

- **Discounts**: You might promote a discount during certain periods, or an exclusive discount on certain solutions, to speed up the products' or solutions' adoption or to clear the shelves to make room for new inventory.

- **Group Discounts**: You might want to offer local companies, or members of certain associations, a discount on your solutions. Think about the discount some hotels offer to AAA members.

- **Buy One, Get One Free Or At A Special Discount**: This type of promotion is often used with commodity solutions, B2C, B2B, and user-based licenses. This promotion can be a great way to offer a new solution, with a discount, that creates a compelling event. The additional purchase increases your revenue, your market share, and, like many of these other promotions, fills another gap in the white space analysis you created.

- **Trade Shows** are an excellent opportunity to meet with your customer base, all in one place. Your sales staff should not think of shows as a holiday, but as incredible opportunities to have formal meetings with a wealth of customers, book back-to-back meetings, and offer some type of promotion. You might consider getting a hospitality suite; having a partner appreciation party; hosting a happy hour for all customers, prospects, and partners to mingle; or conduct executive briefings. Where else can you get such a disparate group of prospects, customers, and your company resources, all in one place, and drive a call-to-action around a specific offer?

- **Internal Sales Promotions**: These types of promotions are internally focused. Maybe you want to drive upselling or cross-selling in a quarter. You might consider internal sales promotions, contests, SPIFs (special performance incentive funds), bonuses, or other incentives that motivate your sales teams, as well as channel and alliance partners, to drive more sales in a given time period. Even though these promotions are not customer-focused, they are effective at increasing sales.

PROMOTIONS

Promotion	Definition	Value to Customers	Range of Potential Revenue	Cost to Offer	Deliverables

Caution: Too many promotions can be confusing, especially if offered at the same time, not only for customers and prospects but also for sales reps.

Offer Innovative Programs

Programs, in contrast with promotions, are typically ongoing and are designed to support customer retention with the added benefit of revenue growth. Programs are particularly effective when focused on the most loyal customers that drive the majority of your revenue.

Below are several programs that you might consider as a way of expanding your customer retention as well as your market share in existing accounts.

- **Early Adopter Programs**: When you have a new solution, you want to help accelerate its adoption. Your satisfied customers are an excellent audience for your new solutions. They are excellent candidates to pilot or purchase your new solutions, and you want customers who want to be the first to use new features that they have been anxious to adopt. In this case, you might offer such programs as white-glove (special care and attention) service for early adopters, which supports them to ensure a great experience. Such a program also benefits the vendor by ensuring any features or bugs are worked out proactively with an understanding customer.

- **Loyalty Programs**: Another excellent way to reward your top customers is with loyalty programs. Loyalty programs are often designed exclusively for your top customers. According to Loyalty Report 2017, the average consumer participates in fourteen different loyalty programs.[47]

---

[47] Ashley Autry, "Customer Loyalty Statistics: 2017 Edition," The Access Loyalty Blog (Access Development, December 31, 2017), https://blog.accessdevelopment.com/customer-loyalty-statistics-2017-edition.

Loyalty programs might be based on a simple point system, or they might include extra discounts, such as those you might receive from Macy's, Bloomingdale's, or Nordstrom. Alternatively, you may offer extra discounts once the customer reaches a certain threshold of purchases, early-bird discounts, and even friends-and-family offers to encourage loyal customers to refer their friends, family, and colleagues to try your solution. Some of the many loyalty programs include American Airlines, United Airlines, Delta Airlines, Marriott, Hilton, Hyatt, Amazon Prime, REI, and Old Navy.

Loyalty programs might also include inviting your top customers to your company luxury box at the closest sports stadium or offering tickets to a popular sporting event. An effective loyalty program rewards loyalty and encourages additional purchases.

- **Newsletters**: Newsletters can be one-time promotions or ongoing programs. Maintaining regular communications with customers is important. What news is relevant to their business? New products and services? New features? New use cases? New industry trends? New awards? Upcoming events? Training events? Industry accolades? Highlights about your company help validate your customer's decision to go with your solution and keep them abreast of what new solutions you offer of which they might not have been aware.

- **Training Programs**: Showing your customers how to get the most out of your solutions is valuable. How can customers derive the most value from your solutions? How can they leverage the advanced features of your solution? These training programs may be in the form of webinars, regional seminars, either targeted at a specific customer or industry, or in a classroom setting onsite or offsite. Sharing best practices, new feature usage, and case studies are often integrated into the training venue to ensure your customers are aware of and getting the outcomes they were seeking to achieve.

- **Referral Programs**: Referrals are the best way to acquire customers because people tend to trust their peers and colleagues. Thus, rewarding your customers to provide referrals is another excellent program. You might offer, for example, a one-month extension, up to a certain value, on their current annual contract, or a thirteen-month renewal instead of twelve-months, for a referral that makes a purchase with your company. We'll talk more about Referral Selling in Chapter Nine.

- **Quotes And Testimonial Programs**: Having testimonials on your website, or that are readily available for sales reps to reference, is worth its weight in gold. Why not offer an incentive to provide those quotes by highlighting them in your next users' conference or including your customer's name in important press events or by providing a software subscription extension? Testimonials include using their logo and quote in your PowerPoint presentations, in proposals, on your website, in a case study, in a brochure, or in a video.

- **Customer Testimonial Contract Program**: You may also want to put a marketing clause in your standard contract that states that you can use your customer's name and logo on your website, in press releases, and other marketing material. Referencing well-known customer brands helps reinforce your credibility in the marketplace. Make this a standard clause that you can always negotiate out.

- **Channel Programs**: The key to a successful partnership is ensuring mindshare within your channel partner community. You might offer perks or programs such as a robust knowledge base, leads, market development funds, or other incentives. You might consider SPIFs that reward selling all of your products or just certain products within your suite of solutions. Trips and contests are also common incentives in partner programs. Channel promotions are vital to the channel because they keep your solutions top-of-mind, which is crucial when you are just one of many vendors the channel partner works with.

- **Alliance Programs**: Leveraging your alliance partners to show the market strength the two of you can deliver to your joint customers helps drive incremental credibility and awareness and, in addition, creates new revenue streams. You might resell each other's products, bundle the solutions, or endorse how well they work together. These programs drive alliance engagement and lead to more sales when customers see the offer as a richly integrated solution.

- **Additional Demand Generation Programs**: There are so many potential demand generation programs. How else do you create demand for your solutions? You might have a formalized executive briefing program at your headquarters. Seminars are another excellent way to drive awareness and create demand. You might consider conducting seminars with your alliance and/or channel partners. Webinars are typically a cost-effective method to deliver consistent, packaged messaging to a large base of existing customers. Plus, you can save these webinars for future on-demand viewing on your website or YouTube. In all of these programs, you can go at it alone, or leverage alliance and channel partners.

- **User Groups And Advocacy Programs**: You might offer regional user groups to drive high engagement across your best customers, which creates a sense of community among users. User groups are an incredible way to bring customers and your internal resources together in one place to share best practices, recommendations, and new solutions. Especially with complex solutions, creating a user community can expand loyal relationships and pay huge dividends.

- **Executive Sponsor Program**: This program maps your executives to the executives of your top customers. If your company utilizes this program, it's key for your executives to maintain regular and strategic contact with the executives with whom they are mapped. Executive sponsorship drives loyalty because customers in the program feel they are getting special attention and have direct access to the vendor's top-level executives.

- **Customer Advisory Boards or Councils**: Customer Advisory Boards (CABs) are excellent vehicles to find out what your top customers are saying about your product while collecting input for future products and services. The focus of CABs is on the customer, but companies benefit greatly as well. An Advisory Group asserts, "Companies benefit from a retention rate of 95 percent amongst program participants, and CAB members are far more likely to recommend their host companies. In fact, CAB member participation in reference programs, testimonials, and thought leadership efforts is 57 percent higher than non-CAB members."[48]

---

[48] Rob Jensen, Ignite Advisory Group, "3 Key Benefits of Customer Advisory Boards for Services Professionals," Technology Services Industry Association (Technology Services Industry Association, May 31, 2018), https://www.tsia.com/blog/3-key-benefits-of-customer-advisory-boards-for-services-professionals.

- **Compensation Programs**: The goal of any incentive program is to drive a certain behavior, most frequently to drive incremental revenue and to create replicable sales activities and results. Incent what you want to be sold with cash or prize incentives, bonuses, SPIFs, or maybe sales trips. In addition to special compensation on certain products, incentive accelerators above sales quota are common programs.

PROGRAMS					
Promotion	Definition	Value to Customers	Range of Potential Revenue	Cost to Offer	Deliverables

This is just a small sample of the many programs that you might implement. The key is to drive messaging, promotions, and programs that drive customer awareness and preference for your solutions.

Real-Life Experience

I've held key roles in sales and marketing, and no matter which function I was in, I worked closely with the other functional area. Coordination is key. First, we came up with a plan. What was the messaging, promotion, or program we wanted to offer? What marketing, messaging, and media did we need? What sales tools did we need to make available for both customers (external) and sales reps (internal)? What testimonials could we leverage? Industry accolades? Alliances? What industry analysts, reference customers, and case studies could we point to, in order to prove our solution delivered value?

Between sales and marketing, we came up with the messaging, promotions, and programs, determined what collateral was needed, and included a few sample emails, voicemails, and social media messages that our customer-facing team members could leverage and deploy proactively. It was important that these messages all tied together in a cohesive, compelling, consistent, and concise message.

As far as specific programs, we sometimes rolled out try-and-buy programs and pilots to increase the usage of new solutions and to reduce the initial risk to the customer. We made trying our solution easy, and we focused on customers for whom our solution would deliver a real tangible result. We also built into the program and messaging an overview of the solution we provided and what outcomes the customer could expect. The key to any pilot or try-and-buy is to ensure exceptional customer support and service to deliver an excellent customer experience. Thus, we also worked closely with customer support and professional services to integrate the offer tightly.

POCs, or bake-offs, were also deployed where, in some cases, the customer had our company and a competitor neck and neck and wanted to compare us in a controlled situation that simulated the real-world application of our solutions. They wanted to see which solution best fit their needs and met their selection criteria. In all cases, we defined the selection criteria upfront, based on our experience of successful POCs. We identified criteria we knew we could meet or exceed expectations, and we highlighted those in the evaluation. We were most successful when we included several criteria that were unique differentiators to our company's product. Just going into a bake-off and hoping for the best is a waste of time, money, and resources for both you and the customer. A well-run POC is a tremendous selling tool, but the upfront definition of success criteria and unique advantages is essential. Offer POCs only if you have a plan to win.

We also focused on trial balloon programs. It is an incredibly effective sales strategy to replicate a consistent and compelling offer that has already exhibited a solid track record of success. To get to that point of a solid track record, you sometimes have to send up a trial balloon, or beta, to test a few things before you get the offer right. I'm a huge fan of trial balloons. Why roll out something that is expensive to implement, hard to pull back on if it's not proven, doesn't yield great results, and gives away too much margin for too little in return? Thus, I'm in favor of asking top customers (or a subset of top customers, advisory councils, or user groups), top sales reps, or channel and alliance partners, which promotions and programs they think are most effective. Plus, the offer works as a trial close, and it invites those participants to feel they are part of the decision-making, because they are. Finally, don't forget to look at what the competition is doing.

Summary

To expand your company's footprint in your customer accounts, you need to enlist the participation and enthusiasm of your marketing team, sales reps, and channel and alliance partners—that is, everyone who is engaged in broadcasting your solutions to your customer base.

To EXPAND your market share in your existing accounts:
- Broadcast your solutions
  – Create compelling external sales tools
  – Brag on proof points
  – Leverage multiple communications vehicles

– Create compelling internal sales tools

- Create persuasive promotions
- Create innovative programs

The next chapter focuses on the "A" strategy of the Land and EXPAND Sales Framework—**A**BPs and QBRs. Understanding your customer's plans will help you understand the best opportunities to EXPAND your footprint in your existing accounts.

CHAPTER 6

A Is For Account Business Plans And Quarterly Business Reviews

"If you don't know where you are going, you'll end up someplace else."[49]
—Yogi Berra

As you read in Chapter Four, on average, loyal customers are worth up to ten times as much as their first purchase.[50] How well do you know your customers? How well do they know you? Do you know what else you can sell to your customers to meet their needs? In this chapter, we will discuss the importance of researching your customers and two important planning processes—the ABP and the QBR.

Journey To Success

Imagine two successful multi-billion-dollar companies. One of them, Company One, had a falling-out with one of their top vendors, and the second company, Company Two, was interested in filling their shoes. The two companies were

[49] Michelle Gorman, "Yogi Berra's Most Memorable Sayings," September 23, 2015, *Newsweek*, https://www.newsweek.com/most-emorable-yogi-isms-375661.

[50] James Macquire, "Customer Loyalty: Using Data to Keep the Love Alive", Experian, June 5, 2018, https://www.experian.com/blogs/insights/2018/06/customer-loyalty-using-data-to-keep-the-love-alive/.

on a mission to define a new partnership to quickly fill the gap. Company Two was the underdog, but a viable option. Their executive management decided to put a full-court press on securing this partnership to replace the incumbent vendor.

Company Two had a zero track record with Company One. And the partnership would require a unique deployment model, different from anything they had ever experienced. Because of Laura's incredible background in opportunities like this, she was hand-selected to lead the challenge. She was looking for someone to work with her who had a strong background in building revenue and a knack for planning and execution to work with her to manage this global opportunity.

I put my name in the hat. This was an incredible opportunity to build a new, large partnership from scratch. The strongest internal candidates were intimidated by the huge quota on this new account, but the account was in my hometown and in my wheelhouse. After all of my strong contenders left the race, I landed the role. Was that a good thing or a bad thing? I was given the largest quota ever in the company's one-hundred-year history.

I teamed up with the lead champion from Company One, and we started by putting together an ABP between our two companies to define their needs and how we could quickly deploy and fill the gap. We needed to go off-site to focus.

We went to Monterey, which is a convenient getaway from Silicon Valley. It wasn't a day off at the beach. It was a serious initiative that required serious planning. Really.

We outlined both of our companies' objectives and put together a comprehensive joint ABP on how the partnership would benefit both of our companies' objectives. The outcome of that weekend was a comprehensive ABP that filled a binder complete with executive maps, initiatives of both companies, and resources that we would align to meet the roll-out.

We submitted the plan to our respective management teams, and the initial ABP was approved. The next step was to get all of the global leaders in both companies to buy in.

Because many of the leaders were avid skiers, we put together a trip for the top executives from both companies to go to Colorado to discuss the plan. Okay, that wasn't a vacation either. Really. Well, we did ski. We needed to create the right environment to be creative, start working as a team, and buy in to this partnership.

The goal that weekend in Colorado was to review the overall objectives of the plan, gain agreement, discuss our annual and quarterly objectives, and then cement our tactical roll-out. Over the weekend, we not only established our joint goals, but we also developed incredible relationships—on and off the slopes—that benefited us during our deployment.

Through account planning with champions from both companies and subsequent executive business reviews (EBRs) between both companies to ensure ongoing alignment, we successfully displaced the prior vendor.

Our partnership achieved over $100 million in annual sales. Together, Laura and I, and all of the teams from both companies, exceeded both company's expectations.

Takeaway: ABPs and EBRs result in incremental sales.

Planning enables you to define the goals you want to achieve and the roadmap to get there. A vital follow-up step is the actual execution of the plan. Pivoting is fine where necessary but planning without execution is a waste of time. Conducting ABPs and EBRs is an essential strategy in defining your joint game plan and getting in lockstep with your customers.

Real-World Scenarios

Consider these two companies.

In the first company, the sales reps hate paperwork. They feel any company or sales leader that requires them to write an account plan has no idea how well they know their customers, and it would be a waste of time. For example, one rep has beers every Friday with one of the contacts, and they frequently enjoy a round of golf. The sales rep believes account plans are a big waste of time and a bunch of unnecessary paperwork that provides a checkmark in someone's box, but it's of no value to his relationship with this customer since they're so well-connected. After all, he has been in sales for twenty years, and he is the master of building relationships. In his own opinion, he has a rock-solid reputation, and he makes his quota most years.

In the other company, the sales rep is focused on being strategic. He works closely with all the members of the customer team, from the champion, to technical, to operations, to the executive staff. His focus is on ensuring he understands their business needs, initiatives, and future direction. He goes to great pains to research the company, its competitors, and the trends in the marketplace that might give his customers a competitive edge; he also considers how those trends align with his company's solutions. He creates an executive map to align his executives with his customers. He puts all of this in his account plan and then validates it with his customer's champion for her input and to determine if there are opportunities for expansion to help his customer meet other strategic initiatives.

The sales rep conducts QBRs, even though they are not required, as he knows it's important to align the executives and show his company's commitment to the success of his customer. The QBRs focus on what's working and what's not; in addition, these reviews validate upcoming initiatives. He keeps a close pulse on his customers' satisfaction. His executives are aligned for an annual round of golf; during the round, they focus on the strategic nature of the relationship and always come back with a lengthy list of actions for the sales team on how to enhance the relationship.

Which sales rep do you think has the greatest probability of exceeding his quota?

Of course, the latter, the more strategic sales rep who focuses on planning, has a far greater probability of meeting and exceeding his plan. The first rep might make his quota, but he has a greater chance of being even more successful with strategy and planning.

Research Your Customers For Insight

Sales reps should look at their accounts as their franchise and themselves as that franchise's CEO. How are they going to grow their revenues based on the accounts or geography that they have been assigned? Sales reps, like franchise owners, have invested their careers and a lot of sweat equity into their accounts. No one wants to fail. The key is execution. But to succeed, you must first understand your customer.

Unfortunately, according to Forrester Research's Buyer Insight study, "Only 13 percent of customers believe salespeople can demonstrate an understanding of their business challenges and how to solve them."[51]

That translates to 87 percent of customers who don't believe a salesperson is doing their job—that is, understanding the customer's pain points.

---

[51] "Why Do Salespeople Fail?," Tenfold, September 16, 2017, https://www.tenfold.com/sales-performance/why-do-salespeople-fail.

Yikes! Sales reps need to understand their customers to be able to sell to them strategically and for their customers to want to buy from them.

According to a sales consulting firm, "Too many people in sales still don't get it. It's not about you. It all starts and stops with the buyer. Good sales professionals are like a doctor diagnosing a patient's illness. If you can't uncover your customer's problems and needs, you don't stand a chance at selling them a solution."[52] How well do you understand your customer and the trends impacting their industry? How well do you know the challenges they are facing? To be an informed sales rep, you should do this research before ever calling on your prospect.

There are many ways to obtain information about your customers. One way is via free information, such as the following:

Free Resources For Prospect Research
- Company website
- Chairman's letter to the shareholders
- SEC documents (annual reports, 10Ks, proxy statements)
- Statement (DEF 14A) for executive compensation and to understand which financial metrics are important
- Analyst reports (both free and fee)
- Investor relations website
- Press releases
- LinkedIn profiles
- Top competitors
- Industry publications

---

[52] Brian Williams, "21 Mind-Blowing Sales Stats," https://blog.thebrevetgroup.com/21-mind-blowing-sales-stats.

Another way to gather information is via fee-based resources.

Fee-Based Resources For Prospect Research

- RainKing, DiscoverOrg, InsideView, Owler, iProfile, D & B Hoovers, BoardEx (sales intelligence databases)
- Zoominfo, Salesgenie, YesData (prospecting databases)
- MarketVision (market research, competition, and trends)
- First Research (industry profiles, industry intelligence tools)
- ProQuest (library news database)

You might have different customer research resources available in your company. For other sources, ask people within your network or within your industry for their recommendations.

Below is a template to document the resources you or your sales reps have at their disposal.

RESEARCH RESOURCES		
Type of Resource	Name of Resource	Free or Fee

After researching your customers, preferably before your first sale, you're now ready to plan how to penetrate these accounts with additional solutions.

Conduct Joint Account Business Plans

An ABP is essential to keep the account team focused on the needs of the customer and the opportunities and game plan to meet those objectives. The better the planning, the better the outcome.

At a minimum, have you identified the elements in the graphic below for each of your top accounts? Do you know the top outcomes, top initiatives, top business objectives, KPIs, and the decision-makers? Do you have a white space analysis?

Do you know what is important to your customers? Do you know how you can provide value and help solve their important problems?

ABPs come in many flavors, and the templates can be home-grown or can be provided by one of the many companies that offer them. A sample of the topics included in an ABP is below.

ACCOUNT BUSINESS PLAN	
Topics	Details
Customer Overview	
Top Customer Initiatives	
Customers Spend/TAM	
Your Solutions Deployed	
White Space	
Decision Makers	
Executive Mapping	
SWOT	
Competitors, Incumbents	
Current Pipeline	
Expansion Opportunities	
New Pipeline	
Risks, Mitigation	
Actions, Owners, Timelines	

The above is just an outline. In your own final ABP, often created in Word or PowerPoint, you'll have a more comprehensive document.

Each of these areas should be validated with each large customer to ensure alignment. Furthermore, it is important to confer with several of each customer's stakeholders to understand the priorities of the company and confirm internal alignment. It is important to address the outcomes important to customers to align your solutions accurately.

ABPs provide a framework and strategic analysis to understand your customer and their needs better. You can develop your own ABP template internally, leverage this sample, or you can access many ABP templates available from several companies on the Internet.

Real-Life Experience

I have participated in account-planning sessions in every company where I have worked. The sales rep responsible for the account did a great deal of research prior to the ABP strategy review by filling in as much of the template as possible. We then brought in a facilitator, such as myself or another person, and several of the stakeholders, including the sales reps, solution specialists, systems or solutions engineers, services, CSMs, industry consultants, and others who were familiar either with the account, the industry, or our solutions.

For our large strategic accounts, we also requested a member of the customer, typically the champion, attend the beginning of our planning session to provide an overview of their company, their direction, top initiatives, and the desired outcomes. In our strategic accounts, customers were linked as strategically to us as we were to them. It was thus of interest for them to be included in these account-planning sessions so that they could provide first-hand input into our planning and explain their strategic initiatives. This cooperation enabled us to map our solutions to their needs.

In several companies, we had sales specialists who supported the sales teams. The sales specialists focused on one solution type and were experts on those solutions. If the sales specialist could not identify how their solution met the customer's needs, as outlined in the ABP, they were not requested to present their solutions to the account. Having a plan keeps you from simply throwing things at the wall to see what sticks, which is not a good strategy.

The goal of the ABP session, besides ensuring an exceptional customer experience from across the organization, was to fill the white space between the desired outcomes or problems as defined by the customer and the solutions that we provided. We then mapped out an action plan with the owners, actions, and milestones for each of the actions.

After the initial plan is completed, the most important subsequent action is to ensure the ABP is a living document with continuous action and refinement against the plan.

You need to project-manage the opportunities identified in the plan actively and make any modifications or adjustments as time goes on.

Ensure Quarterly Business Reviews With Top Customers

Another critical way to stay in touch with customers and identify their needs is to ensure ongoing active communications at the highest levels. QBRs are an effective way to conduct regular reviews with your stakeholders and, importantly, to include the executive sponsors from both companies. These reviews might also be called EBRs, as they might not occur quarterly.

QBRs give you an opportunity to show the relationship is one you value, and to which you are committed, at all levels of the organization. QBRs are an opportunity to discuss the outcomes desired by the customer and how they have been achieved, what's working, what's not, and what you are committed to doing about it. QBRs move you from a tactical relationship to a strategic one and move you toward the goal of being your customer's trusted advisor. QBRs are also an opportunity to discuss the technology roadmap, your recent successes, and accolades such as industry praise or recent strategic marquee logo wins. QBRs, if executed well, are not easy and take preparation time well beforehand. Thus, they are often focused on your top, most important customers.

No matter how formal or informal, QBRs, EBRs, and ongoing communications must exhibit to your customers your commitment to their success.

In the QBRs or EBRs, you not only review how you are solving their problems, but also the uptime and achievement against SLA goals. In addition, a best practice is to first listen to the voice of the customer by asking for their feedback. How is your company performing, what's working, what could be improved, and what's not working? What's their NPS? How likely are they to recommend you to another user? It is critical to take their feedback seriously and to address their concerns. Regular communications result in your not being blindsided.

Key steps to have an effective QBR or EBR:

1. Develop an agenda with your customer champion to ensure the topics meet both companies' objectives for the meeting.

2. Ensure executive sponsors from both your customer and your company participates.

3. Exhibit your commitment to delight your customer and provide an exceptional customer experience.

4. Define and validate the needs and outcomes the customer has identified.

5. Recap the action items at the end of the QBR or EBR to ensure agreement about them.

6. Assign owners, deliverables, and dates to each action item—and follow up on each action item immediately to deliver in a timely manner.

Components of a QBR or EBR presentation might include:

QUARTERLY BUSINESS REVIEW	
Topics	Details
Introduction	Be sure you have the executive sponsors from both companies, and the key players from both customer and vendor, who are directly involved in the ongoing relationship.
Voice of the Customer	Results from last QBR / Customer Satisfaction Survey.
Actions from last Customer Satisfaction Survey / last QBR	What actions have you taken / completed / are in play?
Outcomes / Goals / Results	What were the outcomes proposed or promised, and what are your achievements to date / metrics?
KPIs/ Goals / Results	What were the customer's KPIs, Goals and what are your results against those goals to date?
SLA / Service Metrics / Results	Key is to meet SLA requirements, or to remedy any outstanding issues / goal is to highlight positive results.
Recent News / Trends	Are there relevant trends or best practices that you can share, that show you as a trusted advisor?
Best Practices	Share best practices of other companies in their industry with your solutions, that they might benefit from.
New Promotions / Program	What new promotions or programs are in play, that might be of value to this customer?
Roadmap	What's new / coming?
Other Areas of Interest	What other areas would be of interest to your customer, such as industry accolades, competitor updates?
What's working / What's not? Survey	End with another request for feedback, how do you compare to the competition, what are you doing better, how can you improve, as your goal is to delight your customers—be sure to thank them and tell them how much you appreciate them!
Actions / Owners / Dates	Take actions / and review them at the end to be sure you've captured all open items. Act on these immediately. Don't wait until your next QBR to deliver. But do review their completion / success in your next QBR.
Next Steps	Are there any other areas where you can best support your customer?
	Topics may vary. Key is flow, run it by your champion in advance. Exhibit you've listened to their needs and how you have performed. And continue to deliver exceptional customer service and an exceptional customer experience.

Real-Life Experience

On many of the sales teams I worked with, we focused on large, complex customers. QBRs were table stakes with our top customers. It was absolutely essential to bring our customer's key stakeholders and our company's key stakeholders together to ensure we were meeting the customer's expectations. If there were issues, then we addressed them and showed the customer our commitment to ongoing strategic support.

Having a QBR was critical for us to meet the needs and requirements of the customer on a regular basis, and to understand the many different needs and decision-makers within the organization. These reviews often led to referral opportunities or incremental pipeline for each customer. We focused on timely responses to all outputs of the QBR. We created an action, owner, and deliverable timeline for all of the topics discussed. By maintaining regular QBRs and ensuring executive face time, we were able to improve our strategic relationships consistently to meet and exceed expectations and to grow our footprint in our top accounts continuously.

Summary

Understanding your customers, their top initiatives and the outcomes they are looking to achieve, will put your company in the trusted advisor category as you help them solve key business problems. To understand and address your customers' needs fully, it is critical that you:

- Research your customers for insight
- Conduct joint ABPs for alignment, including champions and key stakeholders
- Ensure QBRs or EBRs with executives from your top customers

- The above steps will help ensure that you become and remain a valued and trusted partner who helps the customer meet its strategic business initiatives. This, in turn, positions you well for a long-lasting and mutually beneficial business relationship.

In the next chapter, we'll discuss the importance of customer feedback in expanding your footprint in your existing accounts. The next chapter focuses on the "N" strategy of the Land and EXPAND Sales Framework—**N**PS and CSAT surveys.

CHAPTER 7

N Is For Net Promoter Score And Customer Satisfaction Surveys

"Spend a lot of time talking to customers face to face. You'd be amazed how many companies don't listen to their customers."[53]
—Ross Perot

Companies that focus on CSAT surveys learn what concerns customers have so they can resolve them. They also learn what new product features and solutions they are interested in, and sometimes they provide great ideas for future products. Would you be surprised to learn, according to Bloomtools, seven out of ten of your customers will leave you because they perceive you don't care?[54] Following up on the NPS and CSAT surveys and resolving customer's issues shows the customer you care and leads to higher retention, loyalty, referrals, and more sales.

---

[53] Blake Morgan, "101 of the Best Customer Experience Metrics for Your Business," April 3, 2019, *Forbes* (Forbes.com) https://www.forbes.com/sites/blakemorgan/2019/04/03/101-of-the-best-customer-experience-quotes/#7e6ddc1a45fd.

[54] Tracy Voyage, "68 of All People Leave a Business Because of Perceived Indifference – What Are You Doing to Keep Your Clients," Bloomtools.com, October 6, 2015, https://www.bloomtools.com/blog/68--of-all-people-leave-a-business--because-of--perceived-indifference----what-are-you-doing-to-keep-your-clients-.

Journey To Success

The company I worked for compensated sales reps to get the surveys completed, and often the highlights or lowlights were included in the sales rep's annual performance review. Completion of the surveys was a big deal. Little did management know, the sales reps could be requesting survey responses from family, friends, or drinking buddies in the account.

The sales rep is just responding to compensation. He's meeting the metric and ensuring a good rating on his performance review. The bottom line is, those glowing but often fabricated remarks swayed the overall results and defeated the purpose of getting real feedback.

To make matters worse, once surveys were completed, the reports went to management, but sales reps rarely heard about them again, good or bad, and customers heard crickets in regard to their feedback.

They brought in Scott, a new executive at the company who was focused on follow-up. He had an incredible background with a major consulting organization, and his micro-focus was on delivering the needs and exceeding the expectations of his customers.

He sent out the results of the surveys, keeping all of his leaders abreast of the responses, by team, so we could compare our teams against each other. And he put together cross-functional team meetings to ensure everyone in the company was aware of what we needed to do, as employees, to address the customer's concerns.

There was one team under his leadership that was particularly lax, and their sales results were not growing as the company expected. They had been operating with a lot of flexibility. He asked me to take over the team and not only expand revenue, but to also enhance the culture to embrace the best practices of putting customers first, listening to customers, responding to customers, and meeting, and better yet exceeding, their expectations. The goal was by exceeding our customers' expectations, we would also be in a better position to grow our sales more quickly.

We put best practices in place to request surveys from a list of executives (not friends) in our top accounts. When I received the survey results back from Scott, I set up regular meetings to share the results with the team. The team went through the results: us compared to the rest of the company, better and worse. We selected the top responses and put a tiger team on addressing the issues, and we got back with the customer on what we were doing to resolve their issues. Most importantly, we followed up regularly on our progress.

By making follow-up with customers the next step, it was clear to our customers that we cared about their feedback, and we reduced being part of the statistic from Bloomtools that 70 percent of customers think their vendors don't care.[55] Many customers were unexpectedly pleased when we diligently followed up because it wasn't the norm with our competitors. The fact that we were following up with our customers meant a great deal to them. Instead of just being a vendor, they began to see us as a partner.

As valued partners who focused on improving our relationships and meeting the needs of our customers, we were rewarded with incremental business. Scott's, my, and the entire team's focus was on being customer advocates, listening to customers, and exceeding their needs and expectations. That

---

[55] Tracy Voyage, "68 of All People Leave a Business Because of Perceived Indifference – What Are You Doing to Keep Your Clients," Bloomtools.com, October 6, 2015, https://www. bloomtools.com/blog/68--of-all-people-leave-a-business--because-of--perceived-indifference----what-are-you-doing-to-keep-your-clients-.

resulted in high satisfaction ratings, as well as exceeding the sales quota. We went on to quadruple our sales in two years.

Takeaway: focusing on requesting and following up on NPS and CSAT surveys to exceed expectations, leads to EXPANDed sales.

Customer feedback is essential. According to *Understanding Customers* by Ruby Newell-Legner, "A typical business hears from 4 percent of its dissatisfied customers."[56] In Chapter Three, I noted, "96 percent of customers don't voice complaints ... [and] 91 percent of customers will never come back."[57] Following up early and often with customers is vital, before it's too late.

Real-World Scenarios

Let's compare these two companies.

The first company sends out CSAT surveys once a year. The company pushes the sales reps to get the surveys completed and even pays a bonus if the sales reps meet the goal of surveys completed. It doesn't matter who answers the surveys, as long as the sales reps get a response from each large customer. Sales reps with good friends in the account get their buddies to fill out the surveys and give high marks, which also results in high ratings for the sales reps in their annual performance reviews. There's no metric to follow up on the surveys, so the sales reps don't follow up. Customer follow up is not a metric, and who wants another metric? The sales rep assumes someone else will follow up on the surveys, and the company assumes the sales reps will deliver the good and the bad results to the customers

---

[56] HelpScout, "Customer Service Facts, Quotes & Statistics How Your Business Can Deliver With the Best of the Best, http://qualitymanagementinstitute.com/images/hrsolutions/Help-Scout-CustomerService.pdf.

[57] Colin Shaw, "15 Statistics That Should Change the Business Worlds – But Haven't," Beyondphilosophy, June 10, 2013, https://beyondphilosophy.com/15-statistics-that-should-change-the-business-world-but-havent/.

so the company can exhibit true transparency. Did I mention the sales reps don't have metrics to provide any follow-up to their customers after the survey, so to them, it's not a priority? Salespeople dislike any more administrivia than is required, and this company doesn't want to demotivate their reps or negatively impact their productivity. The company's perspective is, "We're better off having our sales reps focused on closing the next sale." No one is communicating to the customers that their issues are important or that they were addressed. The issues are eventually fixed, so what's the point?

The second company conducts customer surveys twice per year, and it has metrics in place for the sales reps to have the surveys completed by the top customers by a certain date. This company provides the names of senior executives who should be targeted to request feedback. The company has a team at corporate who consolidates the feedback, assigns teams within the functional departments to address and resolve the issues, and communicates their ongoing status back to sales.

This company takes feedback seriously and wants to be transparent to their customers about what's working, what's not, and all of the "top" activities across the company, as well as those specific to the customer. The company's feedback provides ongoing communications to the customer that their input is not only appreciated, but their feedback is given attention at the highest levels, and the sales reps are measured on ensuring they provide feedback and a satisfactory resolution to the issues the customers raise. The sales reps take great pride in their company's commitment to customer satisfaction and their ongoing quest to ensure the customers' issues are resolved expeditiously. The sales reps aren't compensated to communicate the results, but the sales reps know if they satisfy their customers, they increase the rate of retention and encourage repeat purchases. Sales reps and sales management include the survey results in their communications with customer management and address the results in formal meetings with senior executives from the customer.

Which company do you think will expand their sales faster? Correct—it's the second company. They are focused on not only collecting feedback but making sure they get back with the customer to address and resolve any concerns.

The Importance Of Conducting And Following Up On Customer Satisfaction Surveys

Do you ask for feedback? Do you know what customers think about your company, your solutions, and your support?

How customer-friendly and effective are your chat or hotline personnel? Your onsite technicians? Everyone makes an impression on customers, especially when a customer is dissatisfied with an issue. Ensuring everyone is measured on extraordinary customer support is essential to making that level of support a part of your company's culture.

I've seen too many companies who take conducting the surveys seriously, but then either don't do anything about them or don't bother to communicate back to their customers what they are doing to address their concerns.

The Importance Of Follow-Through

As important as it is to ensure your sales reps request this feedback from their customers, it is equally important that you act on the surveys. Taking surveys is not enough. The customer needs to know you are taking their feedback seriously and that you have a passion and commitment to take positive corrective action. Survey results can give you valuable insight into the customer's wants and needs and, potentially, ideas for future features or products. There is a lot you can learn if you're listening.

It's great when a company takes action proactively, but these steps might be overlooked by the customer if they are not aware or informed that you care. Customers need to know you are taking the steps necessary to make your company an even better partner to them. Let them know what corrective actions your company is taking.

What You Can Learn From Surveys

The components of your survey may be wide and varied. Below is an example of nine questions from HubSpot that you might want to ask.

1. How often do you use the product or service?
2. Does the product help you achieve your goals?
3. What is your favorite tool or portion of the product or service?
4. What would you improve if you could?
5. In your own words, describe how you feel about (insert company name or product here).
6. How can we improve your experience with the company?
7. What's working for you, and why?
8. What can our employees do better?
9. Do you have any additional comments or feedback for us? [58]

Conduct Net Promoter Score Surveys

Your customers' willingness to refer you to others is a key indicator of the impact that a customer's recommendation can

---

[58] Ruchika Sharma, "16 Excellent Customer Satisfaction Survey Examples," The HubSpot Customer Service Blog, accessed March 4, 2020, https://blog.hubspot.com/service/customer-satisfaction-survey-examples.

have on your business—good or bad. What is an NPS? Just how important is it?

According to a source, "Fred Reichheld developed the NPS as a consumer happiness metric in 2004. Basically, NPS uses one question, 'How likely are you to recommend us to a friend or family member?' to gauge the satisfaction of customers and growth of the business. This is the 'ultimate question' to ask customers in assessing a business's potential for future success."[59] The NPS question is simple, but the information you gather from your customer's responses could have a significant impact on your company's growth strategy and trajectory.

According to Bain and Company, "Analysis shows that sustained value-creators—companies that achieve long-term profitable growth—have Net Promoter Scores two times higher than the average company. And Bain's Net Promoter System leaders, on average, grow at more than twice the rate of competitors."[60]

What You Can Learn From The Net Promoter Score

The NPS answer options are arranged horizontally on a scale from zero to ten, based on the following question:

"How likely are you to recommend us on a scale from zero to ten?"

◄ VERY UNLIKELY								VERY LIKELY ►	
1	2	3	4	5	6	7	8	9	10
○	○	○	○	○	○	○	○	○	○

---

[59] "The Importance of a Net Promoter Score and Why It Matters to You," Gravie Blog (Gravie), accessed March 4, 2020,

[60] "Measuring Your Net Promoter Score," Bain, accessed March 4, 2020, https://www. netpromotersystem.com/about/measuring-your-net-promoter-score/.

There are three categories of responders, "promoters," who gave a score of nine or ten, who are happy; "passive," who gave a score of seven or eight; and are satisfied but not enthusiastic, and "detractors," who gave a score of zero to six, who are unhappy.

NET PROMOTER SCORE	
Promoters	Respondents who gave a score of nine or ten
Passive	Respondents who gave a score of seven or eight
Detractors	Respondents who gave a score of six or less

What does the NPS mean, and what should your company do about the results? Bain & Company states, "Your Net Promoter Score is simply the percentage of promoters minus the percentage of detractors … It helps everyone focus on the twin goals of creating more promoters and fewer detractors. It is, quite simply, your customer balance sheet.

Promoters (9 to 10)

Promoters are loyal, enthusiastic fans. They sing the company's praises to friends and colleagues. They are far more likely than others to remain customers and to increase their purchases over time. Moreover, they account for more than 80 percent of referrals in most businesses. They are, in general, pleasant for employees to deal with.

Passives (7 or 8)

We call this group 'passively satisfied' because this group is satisfied—for now. Their repurchase and referral rates are as much as 50 percent lower than those of promoters. Their referrals are likely to be qualified and less enthusiastic. Most telling: If a competitor's ad catches their eye, they may defect.

Detractors (0 to 6)

Detractors are unhappy customers. They account for more than 80 percent of negative word of mouth. They have high rates of churn and defection. Some may appear profitable from an accounting standpoint, but their criticisms and bad attitudes diminish a company's reputation, discourage new customers and demotivate employees."[61]

The key is to not only ask for feedback but to embrace it, share the feedback across functional areas—and do something about the customer's response. Is your customer delighted? Are they comfortable referring you to someone else? If not, what more does your customer want and need from you? What can you do to improve those scores? You need to focus on enhancing the overall satisfaction of any customers who rate you an eight or less, and definitely those with a rating of six or less!

Ask Your Promoters For References

NPS provides you with the customer's willingness to refer you to someone else. It is important to repeat, according to Bain, promoters account for more than 80 percent of referrals in most businesses.[62] As you'll see in the upcoming chapter, referral selling is the most effective way to get new customers (such as new divisions or departments, as well as upselling and cross-selling across an organization). If the promoters are willing to reference your company, don't be shy about asking for referrals (we'll cover this in more detail in Chapter Nine). Every company should focus on how to increase its NPS scores into the nine to ten range.

---

[61] "Measuring Your Net Promoter Score," Bain, accessed March 4, 2020, https://www.netpromotersystem.com/about/measuring-your-net-promoter-score/.

[62] "Measuring Your Net Promoter Score," Bain.

Emphasize Exceptional Customer Satisfaction Through Incentives

Since customer satisfaction is so critical, it is important to measure it. Many companies put annual bonuses or management by objectives and sales managers' objectives in place for sales and others with a direct relationship with customers. By measuring improvement period over period and focusing on high NPS scores and overall high customer satisfaction ratings, you will encourage the behavior you are seeking.

However, customer satisfaction is not the sole responsibility of just sales or those on the CST. It is vital that every department, from your contact center to engineering to manufacturing to operations to legal and every other department, focuses on the customer because every company has an important goal: to grow. To do that requires satisfied customers. Everyone in every department who interacts with customers should have a customer satisfaction goal. In many cases, employees will have a goal in their annual performance review that relates to achieving high customer satisfaction ratings and being proactive and timely in addressing customer concerns. Every employee in every company can make a difference in going the extra distance to create a positive customer experience.

It is critical to measure CSAT and NPS. As you can see from the sample of CSAT and NPS questions, you will learn a lot about how well you are providing customer service and delighting your customers. Don't just go with your gut. Instead, validate you provide excellent customer service with frequent and legitimate customer surveys. Take the actions where there are shortfalls and notify your customers that you appreciate their feedback. Let them know you are committed to addressing any issues or problems by offering solutions to address their feedback and providing an extraordinary customer experience.

Real-Life Experience

Conducting CSAT and NPS surveys was a standard business practice in the large companies I worked for, but unfortunately, such surveys were given only sporadically by the smaller companies. The opportunity was in not only conducting the surveys but in responding proactively by taking action by each group—versus only at the corporate headquarters—and in taking the feedback and acting on it with each customer. Our key differentiator was to always respond to our customers with the specific actions we had taken to address their feedback.

We averaged the survey responses for the highest and lowest responses and shared the results with our customers. Our goal was to be transparent. We wanted to have them see not only where we excelled, but also, importantly, where we had shortcomings and what we were committed to doing about those shortcomings.

At the corporate level, we were provided the overall company scores by question, and our team was compared to the company or the division. This information allowed us to see where we, as a team or division, were excelling or falling short and gave us the opportunity to take corrective action.

The key was to communicate our successes as well as our opportunities to improve in the eyes of our customers. This communication also showed our candor, transparency, and open commitment to improve and differentiate ourselves above the competition. By following up with our customers, we became their trusted advisors, a relationship which led to incremental sales.

Summary

Not only proactively asking customers for their feedback but also showing them that you care by acting on that feedback, and communicating your actions back to your customer, will propel you above the majority of your competitors.

To EXPAND your revenues with existing customers:
- Conduct, measure, and review customer satisfaction
- Take action on the feedback you receive and follow-through
- Share your actions and progress with your customers
- Conduct NPS surveys
- Focus on improving NPS ratings of eight or below
- Ask your promoters for referrals
- Emphasize your commitment to customer satisfaction through internal metrics and incentives

There are foundational areas to ensure customer retention. One is to provide exceptional customer service and an exemplary customer experience; the other is achieving customer delight. Customer delight has become table stakes in today's competitive marketplace. The next chapter focuses on the "D" strategy of the Land and EXPAND Sales Framework—**D**elight your customers daily.

CHAPTER 8

D Is For Delight Your Customers Daily

"Don't just satisfy your customer, delight them."[63]
—Warren Buffett

You must delight your customers to remain competitive and to grow market share. Times have changed, and the quote above speaks for itself from one of the richest and most successful businessmen of our generation—you must delight your customers to remain competitive and to grow market share. What company wants to be satisfied when they can be delighted?

Journey To Success

There was a $6 billion company that had market-leading products. Karen had just been brought into the company to lead the United States sales team, which consisted of three regions. Karen had a solid track record in her prior roles, and she had worked with many of the executives at a prior company. She was known for her ability to deliver top results.

One of her three newly acquired regions had been woefully underperforming. They had not only consistently missed their

---

regional quota; they were consistently the worst of the three sales regions in the US. In fact, I later found out they had missed their quota for the past five years.

Karen asked if I could help turn things around, and I jumped at the opportunity. I enjoy a challenge. There was only one direction to go: up. My personal goal was to not only make quota but to advance the team from worst to first.

I began asking questions. I asked my team, "What's working? What's not?" I also asked my colleagues and leadership the same questions. And most importantly, I asked our customers, "What's working, what's not, and how can we be your best vendor?" The results that came back clearly showed their opinion of us was ho-hum.

One of the first things that we worked on was delivering exceptional service. We worked closely with our services team. We asked what the issues were, what were the outstanding open tickets, and if there were any outstanding concerns or problems that we could assist with. Collectively and proactively, we addressed the customers' questions and concerns and responded more expeditiously. Our customers were delighted with the new, quick resolution we put in place, and they began feeling that we cared.

We also needed to help our customers get the most value out of their current installations. To do that, we reached out to the solution specialists in our organization to set up meetings to help our customers achieve maximum value from our products. In the past, these specialists had been underutilized. We offered to do health checks. We brought the specialists to every customer where it made sense. The goal was to ensure the customers met their objectives, learned best practices, filled any gaps in training, and utilized all of the capabilities of our company's solutions. Having access to our solution experts gave them more confidence in our products, and they subsequently asked what other solutions we had to meet their needs. Sales went up.

We also regularly requested ongoing feedback through EBRs and surveys, not just annual surveys, but each time we met with our customers. We repeatedly asked, "How are we doing? How can we serve you better? What's working, what's not, what can we do better?" The customers saw a vendor who was focused on meeting and exceeding their needs. When they saw a trusted partner who aligned resources to ensure their needs were met, they gained more assurance in our ability to deliver. They gained confidence in expanding their purchases from us across our wider solution suites.

We delighted our customers so much with exceptional service, high-value solutions, and action on their feedback, that we not only met our quota for the first time in five years, we exceeded it. And even better, we catapulted ourselves from the worst-performing team to the number-one sales region out of three in the US that year. Karen and I, and the entire team, had turned around the five-year spell on her worst-performing region. Together, we turned ho-hum customers into delighted customers.

Takeaway: To expand sales, you need to continuously delight your customers.

Delighted customers buy more!

Real-World Scenarios

Let's consider these two companies.

Company A is a startup, and it is short on staff. It is doing the best that it can to stay afloat, and it has an awesome product. It is looking for the next round of funding, and there is incredible pressure on the sales team to close more deals. It is building up a support team but hiring has been slow. It is more focused on hiring sales. Closing more deals is the more critical milestone to get additional funding. Management is stretched thin, so they squeeze sales rep interviews in everywhere they can, but support interviews are taking a back seat. The budget is tight, so QBRs have been postponed, and conducting CSAT surveys is slated for next year when the marketing team is built out.

Company B is also a startup. It, too, is looking for funding from investors and has a goal to IPO or be acquired in two to three years. Its product is positioned well in the marketplace. It needs to drive sales, but it also understands that by delighting customers, it will have a higher probability of retaining the new customers they sign. Executives and sales know customers tell their colleagues about their experience, good or bad, with the company's product or service. Company B goes out of its way to ensure it is delighting its customers with extraordinary support. Company B executives are focused on staffing up both their sales and support teams but have put more focus on staffing up the support team as it will have a more immediate impact on the customers that the company needs to delight. Corporate executives have developed close relationships with all of the new customers so they can keep in touch with them, gather their feedback, and ensure the company is meeting their needs. When necessary, Company B puts engineers on support issues until it can staff up its support team. The company realizes delighting its customers will increase their retention and position them for additional solutions coming out later in the year, as well as provide glowing referrals.

Which of these two companies has a higher probability of expanding long-term revenue? Correct: Company B. Company A is short-sighted, while Company B has a higher probability of long-term success.

Customer delight is exceeding a customer's expectations to create a positive customer experience with a product or brand. By going above and beyond to create a memorable customer experience—fostering an emotional connection and sense of goodwill among customers—will make them more likely to be loyal to your brand long-term. Delight is the process of providing a remarkable experience to users through focusing on their needs, interests, and wishes. The goal of delight is to leave these people so satisfied and happy that they go out and sing the praises of your brand.[64]

Customer Delight Versus Customer Satisfaction

Now you may be wondering, what is the difference between customer delight and customer satisfaction?

Think about when you were in grade school. There were typically three ratings. "Exceeds expectations" thrilled your parents, and you were congratulated by your parents for being a great student and achieving an "A." A rating of "satisfactory" meant you met expectations, but your parents probably perceived it as you scraped by with a "C" rating. A rating of

---

[64] Sophia Bernazzani, "The Ultimate Guide to Customer Delight," The HubSpot Customer Service Blog, accessed March 4, 2020, https://blog.hubspot.com/service/customer-delight.

"did not meet expectations" was equivalent to getting an "F," and you may have been grounded. What level of satisfaction do you think customers want to receive—exceeds expectations or merely satisfies expectations?

HubSpot goes on to say, "customer delight is the process of surpassing customer's expectations to build a long-term, positive experience around your product or service and brand. Customer satisfaction happens when you simply meet customers' expectations. Although satisfied customers are good for your company, delighted customers are more likely to become loyal customers and brand advocates for your company."

A source states, "The new metric for measuring business success is customer delight. If you're not delighting your customers, the prospect of growth in today's highly competitive, low-growth economy isn't promising."[65]

Every employee in a company should embrace the role of creating customer delight. In *Delight Your Customers,* Steve Curtin states, "When [employees are] asked what their work entails, most employees list the duties or tasks associated with their job roles. Very few refer to the true essence of their jobs, their highest priority at work: to create delighted customers who will be less price-sensitive, have higher repurchase rates, and enthusiastically recommend the company or brand to others. Without this customer focus, all that exists is a transaction—and transactional service does not make a lasting positive impression or inspire loyalty."[66]

---

[65] "5 Ways to Delight Your Customers," Hively, December 20, 2011, http://teamhively.com/699-5-ways-to-delight-your-customers.

[66] Steve Curtin, "Delight Your Customers," Steve Curtin, accessed March 4, 2020, https://www.stevecurtin.com/store/a-bundle-of-delight/.

How To Delight Your Customers

Exceptional customer service and an excellent customer experience are the foundation of customer delight, but specifically, what can you do to delight customers? HubSpot suggests the following:

1. Solve customers' problems
2. Be timely
3. Be helpful
4. Help customers succeed
5. Listen to customer feedback
6. Be enthusiastic
7. Be unexpected
8. Build a community[67] [of similar companies]

All of these actions build a long-term positive experience around your product or service and brand.

It is important that companies don't fall into the trap of thinking that customer delight is entirely up to the sales rep, or the customer success rep, or the person at the end of the customer support hotline—although all of these roles are critical. Everyone in a company must be focused on providing exceptional customer experiences and delighting customers, from the engineering team developing great solutions to the marketing team that creates extraordinary relevant messaging to the easy-to-contact-and-resolve-issues support team to legal to operations to finance, and every other department that impacts customers. The key is for everyone to deliver and rise above your competition.

What are your employees doing to delight customers? Delighting your customers does not have to be expensive. It doesn't have to be a formal program, and it doesn't have to be a

---

[67] Sophia Bernazzani, "The Ultimate Guide to Customer Delight," The HubSpot Customer Service Blog, accessed March 4, 2020, https://blog.hubspot.com/service/customer-delight.

dollar discount; instead, it may be as simple as a surprise "thank you." Your company might be a Fortune 500, B2B, or a B2C company, but many of the following ideas will appeal to many of your customers. They all demonstrate a personal touch that anyone in your company can deliver.

Scott Gerber, author of *Super Connector*, consolidated this list of thirteen ways to surprise and delight your customers that anyone in your company can deliver, including:

1. Writing notes
2. Setting the bar high
3. Sending cookies
4. Providing personal service
5. Getting to know your customers
6. Valuing the little things
7. Being a customer advocate
8. Saying thank you
9. Retweeting customers
10. Treating them to birthday coffee
11. Sending them postcards
12. Remembering important dates
13. Checking in [68]

This list is a great reminder of the small gestures that can make a huge difference.

Express Customer Appreciation

Just as most people value being appreciated, so do customers. According to NewVoiceMedia, feeling unappreciated is the number-one reason customers switch away from products and services.[69] Be sure to thank customers for their business and for

---

[68] Scott Gerber, "13 Ways to Surprise and Delight Your Customers Today," Bplans Blog (Palo Alto Software), accessed March 4, 2020, https://articles.bplans.com/13-ways-to-surprise-and-delight-your-customers-today/.

[69] "NewVoiceMedia Research Reveals Bad Customer Experiences Cost U.S. Businesses $75

being great to work with. This helpful feedback reinforces the valuable relationship the two of you have developed. Often, it's the unexpected gesture that has the greatest impact. Remember to thank your customers.

To delight customers, having a culture of extraordinary customer service must be the foundation. According to research from Dixon, Toman, and DeLisi, published in *The Effortless Experience*, "The true driver of customer retention and loyalty is the ease of getting a problem solved. Delight isn't the foundation of a customer service strategy, but rather a second-order effect. First, focus on consistently meeting expectations and avoiding unpleasant surprises. Then go the extra mile."[70]

Real-Life Experience

Over my career, I have been responsible for a single major account to leading worldwide sales organizations. In every role, delighting our customers was our main focus. The key was "not to sell," but to be the trusted advisor to solve business problems. The sales teams met daily, weekly, monthly, and quarterly to discuss how we were doing in meeting our customers' objectives.

We reviewed what was working, what wasn't, and most importantly, we shared best practices developed across the team; that last part had the most impact on our success and in delighting customers. In several cases, we created portals of

Billion a Year," Business Wire, a Berkshire Hathaway Company, May 17, 1018, https://www.businesswire.com/news/home/20180517005043/en/NewVoiceMedia-Research-Reveals-Bad-Customer-Experiences-Cost

[70] Eli Overbey, "9 Research-Backed Customer Retention Strategies," Help Scout (Help Scout, January 24, 2020), https://www.helpscout.net/blog/customer-retention-strategies-that-work/.

best practices to which the sales reps posted. The more postings each rep made, the greater the recognition they received from the team. (Sales reps are, after all, a bit competitive.)

In sales, you're typically measured on customer retention and revenue growth, so our focus was unwavering in ensuring we were providing exceptional customer service, a great customer experience, and delighting our customers. Beyond sales, however, is where the rubber met the road. Customers expect sales to cater to them. It was when our solutions engineers, professional services, and our product marketing, engineering, and manufacturing associates were openly and enthusiastically available to our customers to ensure we were addressing any concerns and exceeding customer's objectives—then, we made an extraordinary impression. Our solutions were mission-critical, so mission-critical support was required, and that's the level of support we provided. Our highly engaged support and operations teams were also readily available to address any concerns at any time, day or night.

In many companies, we often said it takes a village to close a sale and create a delighted customer. Your largest strategic accounts can be the lifeblood of your company. Providing them over-the-top attention, truly delighting your customers, across your departments, goes a long way in retaining your top customers. Yes, we drove significant incremental revenues in those accounts. Everyone needs to go the extra mile to stand out on top!

Summary

Why would a customer want to be satisfied if they can be delighted? Consider the difference between an NPS score of nine or ten (a promoter of your brand) versus a rating of seven or eight (unenthusiastic) or six or below (unhappy). Consider, according to Accenture, $1.6 trillion is lost due to customers switching due to poor service.[71] Consider that brands will no longer compete mainly based on product or price, but now, according to Gartner, 89 percent expect to compete mainly on customer experience.[72] Why would any company strive to be ho-hum, or merely satisfy customers, when you single-handedly control the ability to delight your customers?

Delighting your customers can be achieved in many ways. The main things to consider are:

1. Deliver the outcomes you promised and which the customer expects
2. Go beyond meeting expectations and exceed the customer's expectations
3. Avoid unpleasant surprises
4. Express customer appreciation by telling customers that you value their business
5. Provide extraordinary service and support
6. Ensure everyone in your company is focused on delighting the customer
7. Go the extra mile whenever possible

Companies receive significant benefits when they delight customers. Delighted customers reciprocate with goodwill, loyalty, additional orders, and referrals.

The Land and EXPAND Sales Framework doesn't stop here. The key to expansion is how can you EXPAND your market share most efficiently and cost-effectively. I emphasized how important it is to focus on your existing accounts, due

---

[71] "US Companies Losing Customers As Consumers Demand More Human Interaction, Accenture Strategy Study Finds," Accenture (Accenture, March 23, 2016), https://newsroom. accenture.com/news/us-companies-losing-customers-as-consumers-demand-more-human-interaction-accenture-strategy-study-finds.htm.

[72] Sujan Patel, "These 6 Companies Are Boosting Growth by Delighting Customers," Entrepreneur (Entrepreneur.com, August 24, 2015), https://www.entrepreneur.com/article/249807#.

to a lower customer acquisition cost and the potential for greater average order value. I emphasized how extraordinary customer service, an outstanding customer experience, and delighting your customers have become table-stakes in today's competitive markets.

The next element leverages your success with existing customers in each of these areas, and it is by far the best, most cost-effective way to generate new business—referral selling. You can expand your business with new departments, divisions, and geographies in your existing accounts. Referral selling is the best way to attract and close new opportunities. In the next chapter, we'll discuss **R**eferral selling—the most cost-effective, highest-close-rate way to EXPAND revenues.

PART 3

Sustaining
Land And EXPAND

CHAPTER 9

Referral Selling

"Loyal customers, they don't just come back, they don't simply recommend you, they insist that their friends do business with you."[73]
—Chip Bell

The Value Of Referrals

Referral selling is an inexpensive and effective way to EXPAND revenues. In this chapter, we'll discuss this incredibly effective way to gain new customers: by referral sales. And where do your best referral sales come from—delighted existing customers to whom you are delivering exceptional service and a great customer experience. Delighted customers provide referrals, which leads to incremental revenue and profit. Joanne Black, author of *No More Cold Calling*, notes, "Salespeople who actively seek out and exploit referrals earn four to five times more than those who don't."[74]

---

[73] Michael Wilson, "Digital Business - The Journey to Creating Amazing Customer Experiences," https://digitalbusinessblog.wordpress.com/2018/04/06/loyal-customers-they-dont-just-come-back-they-dont-simply-recommend-you-they-insist-that-their-friends-do-business-with-you-chip-bell/

[74] Joanne Black, *No More Cold Calling*, July 21, 2012, https://www.nomorecoldcalling.com/why-we-are-so-committed-to-referral-selling/.

Journey To Success

Let's look at a large company that sold software, hardware, and services. The company started up a new division and put a hefty valuation on the group. The division had developed an outstanding set of offers. In fact, the solutions were truly superior to any similar solutions available in the market.

David was brought in as the new global leader for the division. The challenge was the division had signed several new marquee customers, but the growth was nowhere near the target revenue the larger company expected, and the parent company was considering reducing their funding to the new division. David needed to fast track sales. He asked me to join him in working with the sales team to rapidly expand the division's overall market share.

Our strategy was to put a heavy focus in several areas: referral selling, cross-selling, and upselling. In addition to landing new customers, we put a heavy emphasis on our existing customers as the fastest path to generate new revenue.

We continued our focus on delighting our current customers and ensuring an exceptional customer experience. The value of this strategy is combining a great customer experience and delighting customers results in customer confidence, which results in customers buying more, and making referrals. With our current delighted customers, we had already created a positive reputation, and their referrals would help us close new business. We also knew from experience that existing customers were far more likely to purchase additional solutions from our company than new prospects.

We assigned CSMs to each of our existing accounts and worked diligently with our customers to ensure we were exceeding their expectations. Loyal, delighted customers with an overall excellent customer experience were our best targets for additional sales and referral selling.

We created a white space analysis, described in Chapter 4, to understand our customers' potential for expansion. We looked at the deployment of our solutions at each customer. What other key locations within their company might be able to use our solutions? We worked with our customers in creating ABPs and conducting QBRs to determine the expansion opportunities.

We expanded our footprint in the customer's departments of our current customers, and we further expanded our sales in new departments across their companies globally. When we ran into a decision-maker we had not met before, we asked our customers if they could make a referral for us into the new decision-makers.

Referral selling had many benefits for expansion. We bypassed lengthy, cold-calling efforts, and we were provided immediate introductions. The benefit was shortened sales cycles, and referral selling instilled confidence in the new decision-makers, resulting in larger initial purchases.

We accelerated our sales, both within existing accounts and in new accounts, where our existing customers referred us. Referral selling had a dramatic impact on our sales. Our sales went up exponentially. The funding was no longer a concern. David and I, and the entire global sales team, had put the team on an upward sales trajectory.

Takeaway: referral selling is the fastest path to grow sales, and it is based on a foundation of exceptional customer service, a great customer experience, and delighted customers.

Expansion Of The Land And EXPAND Sales Framework

Note the arrows of the Land and EXPAND Sales Framework, extending from the "D" and the "E." Exceptional customer service, a great customer experience, and delighting your customer result in the best way to EXPAND sales—referral selling.

The Land and EXPAND Sales Framework™

| Exceptional Customer Service/ Customer Experience | eXpansion Revenue UpSell and Cross-Sell | Promotions and Programs | Account Business Plans and Quarterly Business Reviews | Net Promoter Score® and Customer Satisfaction Surveys | Delight Your Customers Daily |

REFERRAL SELLING

Real-World Scenarios

Let's compare two companies.

Company A offers exceptional customer support and goes out of its way to delight its customers. The company conducts promotions and programs to maintain a high level of communication with its customer base and makes customers aware of cross-sell and upsell opportunities. One of the company's highly successful programs is a loyalty program, while another is a lead referral program. The company creates jointly-developed ABPs with their customer champion, and it has a project manager assigned to ensure all of its actions are met in a timely fashion. The company conducts QBRs with the executives of both companies, and they develop a joint agenda approved by both executive sponsors from both companies weeks prior to the meeting. The company's NPS scores are excellent, and the majority of the results are in the nine-to-ten range, and it strives to increase its scores if they fall below that range. Company A measures its reps on the number of referrals received, and close rates on those referrals, which are then documented in the sales reps' performance reviews.

Company B also offers pretty good customer support, and it delights its customers whenever there is a big push by management. It conducts a zillion promotions and programs, whether it needs to or not, making its customers aware of every imaginable cross-sell and upsell opportunity and frustrating its customers with spam. It even has quarterly contests to see who sends out the most emails each month to prospects. The sales reps are complacent about conducting joint account plans: no one reads them, so they get to check the box, and they are immediately filed away to gather dust. Sales reps are measured on conducting QBRs each quarter with their top customers, but often schedule them with little notice and with haphazard agendas. Its NPS scores are in the eight-and-nine range, which it feels are great. There is no reason to focus on that area because it meets its minimum threshold. All in all, the company feels it is checking all the boxes.

In these two scenarios, which company do you think will receive the most referrals, as well as additional revenue and profit? Okay, I shook things up to see if you were paying attention. Company A is the winner this time! Company A is clearly more customer focused.

Why else are referrals important?

- According to the *New York Times*, "65 percent of all new business comes from referrals."[75]
- According to HubSpot, "Nine in ten buying decisions are made with peer recommendations."[76]
- In an article in the *Harvard Business Review*: "84% of B2B buyers are now starting the purchasing process with a referral ... Peer recommendations are influencing more than 90 percent of all B2B buying decisions."[77]
- According to LinkedIn: buyers are five times "more likely to engage with sales professionals via warm introduction than cold outreach."[78]
- LinkedIn goes on to report that "87 percent of customers want to be introduced to vendors and salespeople through their network."[79]

Referred customers that are pre-sold on the company or the solution by a person they respect, and trust reduces the education and relationship-building time required with a cold prospect. Referrals can significantly reduce the overall sales cycle time.

---

[75] "Referral Marketing: What Is Referral Marketing?," Marketing Schools (Marketing-Schools.org, 2012), https://www.marketing-schools.org/types-of-marketing/referral-marketing.html.

[76] Aja Frost, "75 Key Sales Statistics That'll Help You Sell Smarter in 2020", HubSpot, https://blog.hubspot.com/sales/sales-statistics.

[77] Laurence Minsky and Keith A. Quesenberry, "How B2B Sales Can Benefit from Social Selling," November 8, 2016 (updated November 10, 2016) *Harvard Business Review*, https://hbr.org/2016/11/84-of-b2b-sales-start-with-a-referral-not-a-salesperson.

[78] "5X More Likely to Engage," LinkedIn SlideShare (HubSpot, July 14, 2015), https://www.slideshare.net/HubSpot/webinar-slides-how-to-keep-sales-cranking-in-the-second-half-of-the-year/14-5XMore_likely_to_engage_with.

[79] "Why More Sales Professionals Are Warming Up to Social Selling," LinkedIn Sales Solutions (LinkedIn, April 2017), https://business.linkedin.com/sales-solutions/blog/sales-reps/2017/04/why-more-sales-professionals-are-warming-up-to-social-selling.

The Incredible Value Of Referrals

HubSpot states, "92 percent of buyers trust referrals from people they know."[80]

Joanne Black, referral selling expert, states, "Every seller agrees that referral selling is, hands down, the most effective prospecting strategy. When you prospect through referrals, you bypass the gatekeeper and score meetings with decision-makers every time. Your prospects are pre-sold on your ability to deliver results."[81]

What is prospecting, and why is referral selling so important to this step? Prospecting is the first step in the sales process. It is identifying potential customers who might be a good fit to hear about your offers.

Black goes on to state when you prospect through referrals:

- You've already earned trust and credibility with your prospects
- You convert prospects into clients at least 50 percent of the time (usually more than 70 percent)
- You land clients who, in turn, become ideal referral sources for new business
- You score more new clients from fewer leads (because all of your leads are qualified)
- You ace out your competition[82]

Dale Carnegie stated 91 percent of customers say they'd give a referral.[83] You read in Chapter Three, on Promotions and Programs, that CAB members are far more likely to recommend

---

[80] Aja Frost, "75 Key Sales Statistics That'll Help You Sell Smarter in 2020", HubSpot, https://blog.hubspot.com/sales/sales-statistics.

[81] Joanne Black, "Referral Selling: How to Get More Referral Sales Leads," Salesforce Blog, August 6, 2013, https://www.salesforce.com/blog/2013/08/referral-selling.html.

[82] Black, "Referral Selling: How to Get More Referral Sales Leads", 2013.

[83] Mansour Salame, "How important are sales referrals for B2B Sales?", Oct. 21, 2014, FrontSpin, https://www.frontspin.com/2014/10/21/important-referrals-inside-sales/.

their host companies. And you read in Chapter Four, on NPS and CSAT surveys, that the NPS survey lets you know how likely your customers are to recommend you to others. The NPS promoters who rate you a nine or ten are willing to refer you to friends and colleagues. According to Bain & Company, "Promoters account for more than 80 percent of referrals in most businesses."[84] Have I convinced you of the value of referrals?

Unfortunately, many sales reps are uncomfortable asking for referrals. According to Dale Carnegie, only 11 percent of sales reps ask for referrals.[85] Just think what an exponential improvement in revenues your company can make by increasing your "asks." So, what's keeping sales from asking for referrals?

Some of the hesitancy comes from the fear of hearing the answer, "No." Yet for sales reps, early in our careers, we were taught regarding cold calling, that for every ten "no's," we'll receive one "yes," so those of us who learned that get excited as we get closer to ten rejections. Really, it's true. It means we're close. It's a numbers game. In other cases, people feel as if they are infringing on the customer by asking for a referral. But with referrals, you should not expect "no's," you should target those customers who are predisposed to say "yes."

The key is to ask those most likely to give referrals at the most opportune times. A great time to request referrals is at the same time that you are delighting your customers and receiving positive feedback. During a QBR that is going well is a great time, too.

Referrals can come in the form of customers reaching out to other contacts to recommend your solutions. In addition, case studies, videos, and general positive statements all are

---

[84] Bain, "Measuring Your Net Promoter Score."

[85] Salame, "How important are sales referrals for B2B Sales?", 2014.

excellent testimonials that provide invaluable feedback to other prospective customers.

Endorsements from colleagues and friends, in conversations or posted to their LinkedIn or Facebook, have significantly more impact than reviews from people they don't know. However, even reviews from people the buyer doesn't know, are more influential than marketing claims.

Let's talk about best practices around referral selling.

Referral Best Practices

In all of the previous chapters, you saw how each strategy of the Land and EXPAND Sales Framework helps you to expand revenue and profit. Referrals are also important, and as you saw in the stats above, referrals are seen as the most cost-effective sales strategy.

Let's focus initially on your existing customers—the ones to whom you've delivered exceptional service, and as a result, are delighted.

Which of your customers have a high NPS score of nine or ten? Which ones have offered testimonials or case studies? Which ones allow you to use their names and logos in your promotional materials? Who is on your CAB? Develop a list of prospective referrals along with the person in your company who is in the best position to ask that customer for a referral.

REFERRALS			
Name	Company, Title	Who is the Best Person to Contact	Ranking A, B, C

Don't limit your list to a few names; rather, go overboard on thinking about potential referrals. Hopefully, you now see how impactful referrals are in your business. However, making a list is just the starting point. How do you go about asking for a referral?

Successfully Asking For A Referral

It may be as easy as when you are conducting your QBR, and the customer says, "You are the best vendor we've ever worked with." You might respond, "Thank you. We strive to delight our customers. In fact, our business is based on referral selling. Would you be comfortable referring us to another department within your company?"

Most delighted customers will say yes (91 percent).[86] Your customers do have day jobs, however, and though they have the best of intentions, you need to make it easy for them to make a referral. You might ask, "Would it be helpful if I wrote a short introductory email for you to tailor to your own style, so you don't have to start from scratch?" Many times, an effective time to make the request is done via a one-on-one conversation, maybe at a break, in a one-on-one phone call, or at lunch or dinner. Make the request personal.

I don't know about you, but when I'm provided with a draft, it's easy for me to edit, put my own fingerprint on it, and finally, I'm gently prodded to make good on my offer. After all, I said I would do it.

Make it easy for a customer who has agreed to be a referral to provide that referral. You might create a number of crisp, concise, and compelling introductory referral drafts for your different solutions that your sales reps can leverage with their customers. The key is to make it easy for your sales reps to ask for and your customers to provide referrals. It's not just up to sales; all employees can ask for referrals, as you'll see below. How else do you ask for referrals?

Where To Find Additional Referrals

Referrals aren't just limited to current customers. Joanne Black has put together an entire practice on referral selling. In her book, *No More Cold Calling,* Black discusses building a referral wheel.[87] Where might you look for additional referrals?

---

[86] Salame, "How important are sales referrals for B2B Sales?", 2014.

[87] Joanne Black, *No More Cold Calling* (New York: Warner Business Books, 2006), 122.

In addition to the list above, you might consider and add to the list: former clients, lost prospects, or even people you meet on airplanes, your children's or friends' parents, people you've met at social or networking events, fellow exercisers at your gym, and service providers. For those contacts that are not customers, you will need to be able to articulate a brief, clear, and compelling value proposition. Your message needs to be so compelling that it makes your contacts think about who they might know who could benefit from the solution that you provide.

Just as you did for customers offering to make a referral, create a set of draft emails for your employees to leverage, in case these emails help your referral contacts to articulate what your company does better. But keep them short, concise, and compelling.

Tracking Referral Metrics

Just by saying you are going to focus on referrals, especially when it's not natural (after all, only 11 percent of sales reps ask[88]), won't make it happen. It is beneficial to set up metrics that measure your referral success and drive the behavior you are looking for. Consider setting up referral metrics in your compensation, bonus, or quarterly incentives.

Black suggests considering the following referral metrics:

1. The number of people you will ask for referrals each week

2. The number of referrals you receive that match your ideal customer profile

3. The number of meetings you have with your referred prospects

4. The number of referred prospects who become customers

[88] Salame, "How important are sales referrals for B2B Sales?", 2014.

5. The length of time it takes to convert a referred prospect into a customer

6. The average dollar value of a referenced customer versus your average sale.[89]

The key is not only to track metrics, but to determine your effectiveness, and how to improve your results.

Real-Life Experience

In one of the large companies that I worked for, we had an excellent offering, and we had bonuses for closing new business for the sales reps. We leveraged marketing to go after new departments; we leveraged marketing development representatives and sales development representatives; and we leveraged our relationships in the account, as well as the industry, and on LinkedIn to create "warm" introductions to new departments. By far, the most effective introductions, and the ones that yielded us the best results, were the referrals from customers.

The best time for us to ask for referrals were when we shared with our customers that our business and success was based on referral selling. The precursor to this request was that we were delivering exceptional customer service, an exemplary customer experience, and delighting our customers.

We usually brought this up after they complimented us on our excellent service, or after we reviewed with them the outcomes we had been successful in achieving for their company. Customers are receptive to helping you by reciprocating for the help you have provided to them. It was most effective to ask when we were in a face-to-face environment, such as a lunch or dinner, when the atmosphere was more relaxed and friendly.

---

[89] Black, *No More Cold Calling*, 63.

If they agreed to be a reference, we always offered to write an introductory referral email for them to make it easier. In some cases, they accepted; in others, they said they'd take care of it. In some cases, the referral was to someone else in their company; in other cases, it was to someone in their network, but at another company.

Whenever my teammates or I were prospecting in a new department of an existing company, we always first looked at who we knew in the account, or who in our network was networked with the key decision-makers within the department. For new contacts, we offered to have them talk to a current user in their company so they could hear the testimonial from them, which is much more effective than a vendor's sales or marketing messaging.

Referrals were a key way to expand our trusted relationship across our customers and with new contacts; these referrals ultimately led to millions of dollars in add-on sales.

Referral Selling Leads to Incremental Prospects

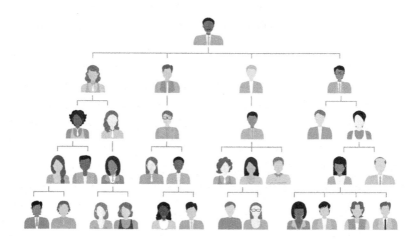

Summary

As noted in this chapter, cold calls require a lot of calls and they are, indeed, cold. A warm lead, such as a warm introduction or referral, goes a long way in improving the reception you will receive from a new contact, increases your chances of closing the sale, and shortens your sales cycle. Referral selling, by far, is the most effective way to prospect for new business, and it exponentially drives up revenue and profit when done effectively.

As mentioned in the introduction and throughout this book, focusing on your current customer base is important to driving incremental sales. Referral selling has the highest probability of gaining expansion in existing accounts. Referral selling should be an ongoing best practice in your sales arsenal.

To be effective at referral selling:

- Make a list of potential referrals
- Ask for a referral when the customer states they are delighted or pays you a compliment
- Ask for a referral if they rated the NPS survey a nine or ten
- Ask for a referral if they are currently offering case studies or testimonials
- Ask for a referral if they are on your CAB
- Ask for a referral at the QBR when things are going well
- Ask others in your network
- Ask if an email referral draft would be helpful (assuming they are willing to make a referral)
- Establish referral metrics

Ask for referrals and you will EXPAND sales.

CHAPTER 10

Looking Into The Future

"Shoot for the moon. Even if you miss, you'll land among the stars."[90]
—Norman Vincent Peale

One goal of this book was to provide you with a robust body of research to give you a broad and varied view of the background leading to the strategies contained in the Land and EXPAND Sales Framework. The second goal was to provide you with real-life experiences of how the implementation of these strategies results in expanded revenue and profit. Lastly, the third goal was to provide you with tips, templates, and checklists that you could put into immediate use in your company.

Summing up the strategies of the Land and EXPAND Sales Framework, the first strategy, "**E**," is based on a foundation of exceptional customer service and an excellent customer experience. Providing an extraordinary customer experience is not only table-stakes in today's competitive marketplace, but it also provides the best ways to retain, and more importantly, to expand your business. Accenture states the estimated cost of

---

[90] https://www.goodreads.com/quotes/4324-shoot-for-the-moon-even-if-you-miss-you-ll-land.

customers switching due to poor services is $1.6 trillion[91]—what is your attrition rate? Retaining customers is critically important. Customers will continue to buy more solutions from you when they have the confidence they will receive exceptional customer service and an excellent customer experience.

Next is the "**X**" strategy. Once you have built a solid customer experience, expansion revenue is the result of cross-selling and upselling—with complementary and upgraded solutions—to meet the additional needs of your customers. According to Nielsen, 50 percent of existing customers are willing to try new products.[92] Have you told your customers about the additional solutions you have to offer that meet their defined needs?

The "**P**" strategy is related to promotions and programs. Promotions are the vehicle to broadcast your solutions to existing customers and create interest in your other solutions that your customers may not be aware of but need, as well as create a compelling reason to act now. Examples of promotions include special offers, such as bundled offers and try-it-buy-it, typically with a timestamp associated with them. Customers, on average, buy ten times their initial purchase.[93] Programs are the vehicles to promote retention in your top accounts. Programs include CABs, loyalty programs, and lead referral programs. These promotions and programs all lead to incremental revenue and profit.

---

[91] "U.S. Companies Losing Customers As Consumers Demand More Human Interaction, Accenture Strategy Study Finds", March 23, 2016, Accenture, https://newsroom.accenture.com/news/us-companies-losing-customers-as-consumers-demand-more-human-interaction-accenture-strategy-study-finds.htm.

[92] "Global Consumers More Likely To Buy New Products From Familiar Brands", January 23, 2013, https://www.nielsen.com/us/en/press-releases/2013/global-consumers-more-likely-to-buy-new-products-from-familiar-b0/.

[93] James Macquire, "Customer Loyalty: Using Data to Keep the Love Alive", Experian, June 5, 2018, https://www.experian.com/blogs/insights/2018/06/customer-loyalty-using-data-to-keep-the-love-alive/.

Next is the "**A**" strategy, which addresses the importance of creating ABPs and conducting QBRs. These two critical planning tools will set you up to understand your customers' additional needs better and learn where you can help them fill the gaps. These essential tools also position you to become a coveted trusted advisor who has earned their confidence. Joint planning with your customers creates a roadmap for addressing future needs for them and future revenue and profit for you.

The "**N**" strategy is related to NPS and CSAT surveys. It is absolutely critical to hear the feedback from your customers about what's working and what's not. NPS and CSAT surveys are formal ways to maintain an ongoing commitment not only to listen but also importantly, to act on their feedback and to communicate your actions back to the customer. In addition to the goal of exceeding expectations, high promoter scores lead to referrals, which lead to incremental sales.

The "**D**" strategy is to delight customers daily. Once you have achieved the pinnacle of truly delighting customers by consistently going the extra mile, well above the mundane level of merely satisfying them, delighted customers reciprocate with goodwill, loyalty, and additional orders. In addition, combined with an exceptional customer experience, you are now in a position to ask for referrals—the best, sure-fire way to increase your top and bottom line.

When you have delivered both of the strategies, exceptional customer service and a great customer experience, and you delight your customers, referral selling naturally occurs. Referral selling is the most cost-effective, highest-close-rate way of driving incremental revenue and profit. The main thing to remember about referrals is: don't forget to ask.

The Land and EXPAND strategies are more important than ever before. To build your business and thrive, incorporating the strategies in this book, particularly in this customer-centric era, are vital.

By embracing these six simple strategies of the Land and EXPAND Sales Framework, you will EXPAND your company's top and bottom line!

Here's to your incredible success!

The Land and EXPAND Sales Framework™

| Exceptional Customer Service/ Customer Experience | eXpansion Revenue UpSell and Cross-Sell | Promotions and Programs | Account Business Plans and Quarterly Business Reviews | Net Promoter Score® and Customer Satisfaction Surveys | Delight Your Customers Daily |

REFERRAL SELLING

LAND AND EXPAND

Strategies	Actions to Execute
Exceptional Customer Service / Customer Experience	1. Focus on feedback 2. Provide exceptional service 3. Make CX a part of your culture 4. Set up a customer centric organization 5. Assess and quantify customer success metrics
EXpand with UpSell and Cross-sell	1. Conduct a white space analysis 2. Increase revenue through upselling 3. Increase revenue through cross-selling 4. Uncover opportunities through communications 5. Increase opportunities through ABPs, QBRs, NPS and CSAT surveys 6. Assess the competition
Programs and Promotions	1. Broadcast your solutions a) Compelling External sales tools b) Brag on proof points c) Leverage multiple communications vehicles d) Compelling Internal sales tools 2. Create persuasive promotions 3. Create innovative programs
Account Business Plans and Quarterly Business Reviews	1. Research your customers for insight 2. Conduct Joint Account Business Plans 3. Ensure Quarterly Business Reviews with your top customers
Net Promoter Scores and Customer Satisfaction Surveys	1. Conduct, measure, and review Customer Satisfaction Surveys 2. Take action on the feedback you receive 3. Share your actions and progress with your customers 4. Conduct NPS surveys 5. Focus on improving NPS ratings of 8 or below 6. Ask your Promoters for referrals 7. Drive behavior through metrics and compensation
Delight Your Customers Daily	1. Deliver the outcomes you promised, and the customer expects 2. Go beyond meeting expectations and exceed the customer's expectations 3. Avoid unpleasant surprises 4. Thank your customer for being a great customer and tell them that you value their business. 5. Provide extraordinary service and support 6. Ensure everyone in your company is focused on delighting the customer 7. Go the extra mile whenever possible
Referral Selling	1. Make a list of potential referrals 2. Ask for a referral when the customer states they are delighted or pays you a compliment 3. Ask for referrals if they rated the NPS survey a 9 or 10 4. Ask for a referral at the QBR when things are going well 5. Ask others in your network 6. Ask if an email referral "draft" would be helpful (assuming they are willing to make a referral) 7. Establish referral metrics

APPENDIX A

Glossary Of Acronyms

AOV: Average Order Value

ABP: Account Business Plan

B2B: Business to Business

B2C: Business to Consumer

CAB: Customer Advisory Board

CAC: Customer Acquisition Cost

CSM: Customer Success Manager

CST: Customer Success Team

ERP: Enterprise Resource Planning

EBR: Executive Business Review

FTE: Full-Time Equivalent

GAM: Global Account Manager

GTM: Go-to-Market

KPI: Key Performance Indicator

LTV: Lifetime Value

MAM: Major Account Manager

NPS: Net Promoter Score

POC: Proof of Concept

QBR: Quarterly Business Review

ROI: Return on Investment

SaaS: Software as a Service

SLA: Service Level Agreement

SMAM: Select Major Account Manager

SWOT: Strengths, Weaknesses, Opportunities, Threats
TAM: Total Addressable Market
VOC: Voice of the Customer

APPENDIX B

Acknowledgments

I would like to thank the following who assisted me in finalizing this book. Special gratitude goes to the individuals below. Your knowledge, expertise, and support were invaluable.

Thank you!

Theresa Marcroft, MarketSavvy, Inc.
Special thanks to my older brother, Garry

About The Author

Patricia Watkins is the Managing Partner of MORE SALES Advisors, an advisory group that works with companies who want to accelerate their sales results.

Watkins has extensive experience as a SVP and VP of Sales, regionally, nationally, and globally at both startups in Silicon Valley and at Fortune 500 companies, including HP, Teradata, AT&T, and NCR.

Watkins has built and led sales organizations from $0 to over $800 million in annual sales and transformed several sales teams from worst to first.

Watkins earned her BBA from the University of Texas at Austin and her MBA from Santa Clara University, both with honors.

For more information on bulk-order discounts of this book or to learn more about hiring Watkins as a keynote or workshop speaker, please e-mail pwatkins@MORESalesAdvisors.com.

For additional information, go to:
www.Land-and-Expand.com
OR
www.MORESALESAdvisors.com

Made in the USA
Columbia, SC
21 September 2020